PRIMARILY for Cub Scouts

WITHDRAWN

JEFFERSON COUNTY PUBLIC LIBRARY

PRIMARILY for Cub Scouts

Trina Boice

CFI
Springville, Utah

© 2009 Trina Boice

All rights reserved.

No part of this book may be reproduced in any form whatsoever, whether by graphic, visual, electronic, film, microfilm, tape recording, or any other means, without prior written permission of the publisher, except in the case of brief passages embodied in critical reviews and articles.

This is not an official publication of The Church of Jesus Christ of Latter-day Saints. The opinions and views expressed herein belong solely to the author and do not necessarily represent the opinions or views of Cedar Fort, Inc. Permission for the use of sources, graphics, and photos is also solely the responsibility of the author.

ISBN 13: 978-1-59955-352-8

Published by CFI, an imprint of Cedar Fort, Inc., 2373 W. 700 S., Springville, UT 84663
Distributed by Cedar Fort, Inc. www.cedarfort.com

LIBRARY OF CONGRESS CATALOGING-IN-PUBLICATION DATA
Boice, Trina, 1963-
  Primarily for Cub Scouts / Trina Boice.
     p. cm.
  Includes indexes.
  Summary: Ideas for cub scout leaders, including lesson and pack meeting
suggestions, activities, and special occasion celebrations. Includes
sections on improving parental support and motivating scouts and leaders.
  ISBN 978-1-59955-352-8
  1. Cub Scouts. I. Title.

HS3314.B55 2010
369.43--dc22

2009039344

Cover design by Angela D. Olsen and Jen Boss
Cover design © 2009 by Lyle Mortimer
Edited and typeset by Melissa J. Caldwell

Printed in the United States of America

10 9 8 7 6 5 4 3 2 1

Printed on acid-free paper

**To my husband and four sons,
who have enabled me to enjoy this wonderful
adventure through scouting.**

**I'm so proud of my boys—Cooper, Calvin, Bradley,
and Bowen—for always excelling in Cub Scouts
and Boy Scouts and for truly living the Scout Law
in word and deed. I love you!**

Contents

Acknowledgments ix

Introduction 1

  1. I Am a Child of God 9

  2. First Presidency Letter 14

  3. My Baptismal Covenant 17

  4. Award Requirements 21

  5. Learning and Living the Gospel 52

  6. Serving Others 58

  7. Developing Talents 71

  8. Preparing for the Priesthood 87

  9. Motivation and Recognition 92

CONTENTS

10. Parental Support **99**

11. Funtastic Traditions **104**

12. Fun Field Trips **111**

13. Den Meeting Do's **115**

14. Blue and Gold Banquet Brainstorm **118**

15. Pinewood Derby **120**

16. Silly Cheers, Skits, and Songs. **123**

17. Pack Meeting Ideas **127**

18. The Religious Square Knot Award. **132**

Appendix 1: Website Resources **136**

Appendix 2: Primary's Faith in God and Cub
Scout Equivalents **142**

Appendix 3: Passing Off Requirements **152**

Index **155**

About the Author. **159**

Acknowledgments

A big thanks to Cedar Fort, Inc., for believing in this book and making it happen! Thank you to my four sons who have given me many happy years of fun Cub Scouting adventures. The Cub Scout program is very sweet and has blessed my life as well as my boys'. Thanks to my husband for being a great Cub Master and father and for being the one to load up all of the camping gear each trip, hike in the snow and rain with our boys, sleep in cold tents, and crawl through muddy caves on spelunking trips.

In 2002 I was given the "God-send Award" by the Boy Scouts of America Council in Georgia where we lived for fifteen years. I should have given them an award for all that they did for my family!

My two oldest sons are now Eagle Scouts, while my third son is currently working on his. I'm happy to say that my youngest son is still in Cub Scouts, so I get to play with the "Blue and Gold" a little bit longer!

Finally, a big thanks to all of you moms and dads who are serving with valiant hearts to feed the Savior's littlest lambs in the Cub Scout program. May you feel the Savior's love as you serve.

Introduction

All I Need to Know I Learned in Primary
—Author Unknown

I am a Child of God.
Believe in Christ.
Do unto others as you would have them do unto you.
Choose the right.
Where love is, there God is also.
Cleanliness is next to Godliness.
Give oh give.
Listen to the still small voice.
Count your many blessings.
Do the things the Lord commands.
Honor your father and mother.
Dare to be true.
Kindness begins with me.
Search, ponder, and pray.
Listen to the prophet's voice.
Jesus said love everyone.
When you're helping, you're happy.

Introduction

> Heavenly Father hears and answers prayers.
> There is beauty all around.
> Reverently and quietly pray.
> Sunday is special.
> Do your duties with a heart full of song.
> My body is a temple.
> Heavenly Father loves me!
> Dare to do right.
> Keep the commandments.
> Pray in faith.
> The priesthood is restored.
> Families can be together forever.
> Jesus is risen.

Remember the conversation Jesus had with Peter about feeding sheep? (John 21:15–17). Before Jesus asked His beloved disciple to take care of His sheep, He said, "Feed my lambs." Now, that may seem like unimportant wording, but to me it sends the message that we need to care for and teach our littlest ones first. They are not to be overlooked in God's kingdom here on earth. We are to nurture them physically and spiritually.

During the first forty-eight years of the history of the Church, the children did not have their own organization. Aurelia Spencer Rogers, a mother of twelve children, was concerned about the rowdy behavior of the boys in her neighborhood. She spoke with Eliza R. Snow, the general Relief Society president at the time, who then spoke with the prophet, President John Taylor. Sister Rogers asked if boys could have their own organization where they could be "trained to make better men." The prophet thought such an organization would be better if girls were also included because he thought they would make the singing sound better! Sister Rogers was called to be the

INTRODUCTION

first Primary president, and in 1878 the first Primary meeting was held with 215 boys and girls "to be taught obedience, faith in God, prayer, punctuality, and good manners."[1]

Over the years the Primary program has evolved, but the purpose has always been the same: to "teach children the gospel of Jesus Christ and help them learn to live it."[2] This purpose is based on 3 Nephi 22:13: "And all thy children shall be taught of the Lord; and great shall be the peace of thy children." Eighth general Primary President Michaelene P. Grassli counseled, "When children are taught of the Lord we bestow on them a gift, a legacy of peace that can lead them to eternal life. We must not fail them."[3] To have faith in God is to have peace. Today, the Faith in God program is the gift of peace we can give our children in a turbulent world.

In addition to working on goals in the Faith of God program, Primary-age boys can attend Cub Scout activities, as well as quarterly Activity Days. All of these activities should provide our precious young boys opportunities to

- Learn the gospel and practice living it.
- Develop good habits at an early age.
- Build gospel-centered friendships.
- Participate in missionary work by inviting their friends to a fun activity.
- Prepare for the transition into the Young Men's programs.
- Prepare for receiving the priesthood.
- Develop a testimony.
- Develop and share talents.
- Keep the covenants made at baptism.

INTRODUCTION

- Serve others.
- Be prepared to make good choices.
- Come unto Christ.

Remember to open and close your Activity Day and Cub Scout meetings with prayer. The purpose of the activities is to develop faith in God, not just have activities! We live in perilous times when attacks on the family have become quite aggressive. We need to fight back harder and protect the Savior's lambs. While Satan has had thousands of years to fine-tune his destroying powers, the young children whom we are called to protect and nurture have lived less than a dozen years here on Earth and are ill-prepared to protect themselves alone. We need to equip them with tools, dress them with spiritual armor, and surround them with love and safety.

In 1979 President Ezra Taft Benson said,

> For nearly six thousand years, God has held you in reserve to make your appearance in the final days before the Second Coming of the Lord. Every previous gospel dispensation has drifted into apostasy, but ours will not. While our generation will be comparable in wickedness to the days of Noah, when the Lord cleansed the earth by flood, there is a major difference this time. It is that God has saved for the final inning some of his strongest children who will help bear off the kingdom triumphantly. And that is where you come in, for you are the generation that must be prepared to meet your God. All through the ages the prophets have looked down through the corridors of time to our day. Billions of the deceased and those yet to be born have their eyes on us. Make no mistake about it—you are a marked generation. There has never been more expected of the faithful in such a short period of time as there is of us. Never before on the face of this earth have the forces of evil and the forces of good been as well organized. Now is the great day of the

INTRODUCTION

devil's power, with the greatest mass murderers of all time living among us. But now is also the great day of the Lord's power, with the greatest number ever of priesthood holders on the earth. And the showdown is fast approaching."[4]

As members of the Church, we often quote this powerful message to the youth, but it also applies to you, their leader!

The Faith in God program for boys is designed to help them learn about the priesthood and become worthy and ready to receive it. The Lord's plan depends on it. When you are set apart as a Primary Activity Day leader or Cub Scout leader, you are given a mantle of authority and the right to receive personal revelation for those whom you serve. Pray to understand the needs of the children. Every boy is unique, and it will be your challenge to touch their lives and hearts. To be an effective leader, you will need to know these boys and understand their challenges.

Prepare yourself in every way as you invite Heavenly Father's precious sons to "come unto Christ." The most important thing you will do is introduce your boys to the Lord and help them want to be like him. As you are prayerful and diligent, many ways to impact and touch their lives will be opened to you.

One thing I learned very quickly on my mission is that my words were not as important as I thought they were. I had competed on the speech and debate team in high school and during my college years at BYU, so when I went on my mission to Spain, I tried to learn the correct vocabulary words I thought would have the most impact. I soon realized that it wasn't my word choice that converted souls to Christ, but rather, it was the testifying power of the Holy Ghost! I realized that the most important thing I could do was to create an environment where the Holy Ghost would be welcome and could touch the heart of the listener. That is your challenge as a Primary worker as well.

You can spend hours planning lessons or activities, but if the children

Introduction

aren't opening up their scriptures and supping from its pages with you, they won't go home filled spiritually. Your activities need to be different than the ones the world offers. Help them learn to love the scriptures and how to pray. These two things will strengthen and nourish their faith for the rest of their lives. Create a loving, supportive, safe environment for your boys so their hearts will be softened and receptive to the testifying witness of the Holy Ghost. More important than feeling their leader's love, the children must feel the Savior's love.

Young boys have plenty of activities that compete for their time and attention. Your role as a leader is not to create yet another activity that parents have to juggle, but to provide a program that truly inspires faith in God, builds testimony of the Savior, and strengthens the family.

When I was a little girl in Primary, I had many teachers who inspired me to be good by what they taught and, more important, by their actions. They taught me gospel principles and gave me opportunities to practice living them. I remember one summer day when my teacher taught a lesson about the Word of Wisdom. Instead of simply presenting gospel principles and ending the lesson with a prayer, she handed a 3x5 card to each of us and asked us to write our commitment to live the law. I still have that card! Throughout my life, whenever I had to choose about whether or not to drink alcohol, take drugs, or smoke, I have easily chosen the right because of the decision I made in a small Primary room years ago with the help of an inspired Primary teacher. I don't remember her name, but I'll never forget how she taught me the gospel and how to live it.

Let the boys know you love the Lord and that you find joy in living the gospel. Provide them with opportunities to apply the gospel in their lives daily as they make choices, go to school, spend time with friends, and live at home. Help them transfer their understanding of the gospel from their head to their heart. While preparing your lessons and activities, prayerfully consider the

Introduction

boys' needs. You are not teaching lessons; you are teaching Heavenly Father's children! His lambs are hungry, and you can nourish their souls.

Before reading this book, you should become familiar with the material the Church has provided you for your calling, such as the Faith in God booklet, the *Friend* magazine, leadership manuals, and the Church's website, www.lds.org. You should also be given a Cub Scout manual. The Cub Scout program is terrific, offering all kinds of fun activities for boys to learn skills, have new experiences, and create wonderful memories with their families.

This book has been organized to easily follow along with the Faith in God booklet, page by page. At the end of this book are additional chapters filled with fun ideas to incorporate into your ward or branch. Every unit of the Church has its own unique personality and needs, so feel free to adapt the ideas to meet the needs of your own Primary. Remember that children thrive when given a mixture of fun and inspirational activities.

Now, don't get overwhelmed when you see the long lists of requirements and ideas in this book! You're not expected to do them all! Find the ideas that work best for your group's specific needs and concentrate on making your activities enjoyable for everyone, including you. This is supposed to be fun!

You will notice that many ideas in the book include a list of the Cub Scout requirements that are fulfilled when completing the activities. These requirements enable the boys to pass off both a Faith in God requirement and a Cub Scout requirement at the same time. Some Cub Scout dens in the Church are small and include boys of various ages and ranks, so when you plan one of the listed activities, you will see which achievements are earned for all of your Cub Scouts!

Whether you serve in the Primary program for a few months or a few years, you will grow closer to the Savior as you develop pure love for his lambs. One of my favorite passages of scripture is when the Savior appeared to the Nephites and commanded that their little children should be brought to him

(3 Nephi 17:11–25). There must have been many children in that multitude, and yet Christ took the time to bless them one by one and pray for them. This is a powerful lesson: each soul is rescued one at a time. Each child was personally ministered to by angels from above.

My heart fills with wonder and love as I imagine what it would have been like to see angels descend from heaven in the midst of fire, encircling those little ones about and ministering to them. Today, you are the angel who has been called to minister to the Lord's littlest ones in his kingdom!

Notes

1. *Encyclopedia of Mormonism*, ed. Daniel H. Ludlow, 5 vols. (New York: Macmillan, 1992), 3:1146.
2. *Church Handbook of Instructions, Book 2: Priesthood and Auxiliary Leaders* [1998], 229.
3. Michaelene P. Grassli, Primary open house, Apr. 2003.
4. Ezra Taft Benson, "In His Steps," in *Speeches of the Year, 1979* (Provo: Brigham Young University Press, 1980), 59.

1

I Am a Child of God

Every Primary child quickly learns the words to the classic Primary song "I Am a Child of God." The activity ideas on the first page of the Faith in God booklet help transfer those words from the tongue into the heart of each child. It is by inspired design that this concept is introduced first in the Faith in God program and booklet. This simple truth will guide each boy for the rest of his life. Plan a day when you can take pictures of each boy to place in their Faith in God booklets. Talk about the words on the inside cover of their booklet and incorporate some of the following ideas into your activities to help the boys really internalize those words.

✦ Go on a nature hike and talk about all the beautiful things the Lord has created, including them! (Wolf Achievement 10c; Wolf Elective 18b, c, e, f; Bear Elective 12a, b, c, e, f, g, h; Webelos Badge Requirement; Webelos Naturalist pin 1a, b, c, 6, 7, 8, 9, 10, 11; World Conservation Award; Arrow of Light 5; Academic Belt Loop for Wildlife Conservation. Webelos who draw or paint an outdoor picture fulfill Webelos Artist 3. If the hike lasts three miles then Webelos can also fulfill Outdoorsman 9)

✦ Discuss healthy habits and why it's important to take care of the body that Heavenly Father has given us. Have the boys cut out pictures from magazines showing foods that are good and bad for their bodies. Draw a picture of a refrigerator and have them put the good food in the refrigerator. Toss the bad pictures into the garbage can. Read the Word of Wisdom and make a list of healthy habits the boys can include in their daily routine, such as brushing their teeth and hair. Do some fun physical exercises together. (Wolf Achievement 1a, b, c, d, e, f, g, j, k, l; Wolf Achievement 3 a, b, c; Wolf Achievement 8a; Wolf Elective 3b; Bear Achievement 11f; Bear Achievement 16a, b, c; Webelos Badge Requirement 5; Webelos Athlete 1–7; Webelos Fitness 1, 5, 6, 7, 8; Arrow of Light 3)

✦ Have a progressive dinner where the boys start in one home to enjoy appetizers, then go to another house for salad, then another house for the entrée, and a final house for dessert. If the families live too far apart in your ward to make this activity feasible, then simply have the boys travel to different rooms in your Church building for each course. At each home have a short lesson on various aspects of their divine nature and compare the progressive dinner to our progression back to our heavenly home. Talk about good nutrition and have the boys help prepare parts of the meal. (Wolf Achievement 8a, b, e; Webelos Fitness 1, 5, 6, 7, 8)

✦ Learn about the song "I Am A Child of God" and its composer. Teach the boys how to conduct it and coordinate an opportunity for them to do so during sharing time on Sunday. Learn to sing it in another language. (Wolf Elective 11d, e; Webelos Communicator 4, 10; Webelos Showman 11, 12, 13, 14; Academic Belt Loop for Music)

✦ Meet Mormon musicians. Introduce the boys to new LDS musicians by playing their music. Write letters or emails to the artists to thank them for sharing their talents and musical testimonies. (Wolf Elective 11d, e, f; Wolf Elective 21b; Webelos Communicator 11, 13; Academic Belt Loop for Music)

✦ Talk about their "sweet" spirits and teach them how to make a sweet dessert or treat. (Bear Achievement 9a, b, d, f)

✦ Decorate shoes, jeans, backpacks or T-shirts to help the boys remember who they are and whose they are. (Wolf Elective 3a, e)

I Am a Child of God

- Learn how to make different kinds of candles and talk about what it means to "wax strong" like in the scriptures. (Wolf Elective 3 a, e)

- Talk about nature and the Lord's handiwork, emphasizing that we are His greatest creation. Teach the boys various kinds of "handiwork" such as crocheting, cross-stitch, knitting, and tatting. It's not just for girls! Have them write "I Am A Child Of God" on their project, using a new stitch they have learned. (Wolf Elective 3a, e)

- Talk about how the Church magazines help us remember who we are. Spend time sharing stories and projects from the *Friend* magazine. Have each boy come to the den meeting with a story, game, poem or recipe from the *Friend* to share. (Wolf Elective 22c; Webelos Showman 1, 16)

- Go to a local planetarium and learn about this incredible universe Heavenly Father has created for us! Many local colleges have free shows and observatories you could visit. Talk about how each boy plays an important part in the plan. (Bear Elective 1a, e, f)

- Hold a "Tacky Night" where everyone comes dressed in tacky clothes, eats tacky food (Spam, beans out of a can, and so forth). Talk about how to dress and behave in a "classy" manner that is becoming of someone who truly has divinity within them. Talk about the importance of respect, good grooming, and attire for those who hold the priesthood and perform its ordinances. (Wolf Achievement 7a)

- Make photo albums and talk about how important the boys' lives are to Heavenly Father. Show some scrapbooking techniques as well. (Wolf Elective 3 a, e; Webelos Artist Badge 2)

- Decorate journals, and talk about how writing can be therapeutic, enabling us to see our potential and to remember we are children of a loving Father in Heaven. (Wolf Elective 3a, e; Webelos Artist Badge 2)

- Talk about what a blessing our families are. Share ideas of their favorite family home evening lessons. Prepare a lesson the boys could use next week at home with their families, including visual aids, a refrigerator magnet, and a recipe for refreshments. (Webelos Family Member 1; Webelos Showman 1, 16)

✦ Teach the boys about genealogy and talk about how we inherit physical and personality traits from our parents. Help them create a photo pedigree chart for their family. Then talk about the traits we receive from our Heavenly parents. (Webelos Family Member 1; Heritages Belt Loop)

✦ Have the boys create a poster or bulletin board to display in the Primary room that reminds all of the children that they are children of God. (Wolf Elective 3a, e; Wolf Elective 12a, b, d; Webelos Family Member 1)

✦ Encourage the boys to help each other identify why they are special by having them write down positive character traits they see in others. Pass around a piece of paper with each boy's name on it and take turns writing and passing the papers around until everyone's page is full of kind words! (Bear Achievement 18b; Bear Achievement 24d, f)

✦ Invite the Young Women in your ward to share a special presentation with the boys about one of the values in the Young Women's program: Divine Nature. They're sure to have lots of great ideas! (Wolf Achievement 11a, c; Bear Achievement 1a, b)

✦ Cut out paper letters that spell "I Am a Child of God" and hide them around the room. Invite the boys to find the letters and figure out what it spells. Talk about how sometimes it takes a lot of searching for some people to realize how special they are! (Wolf Elective 18c; Bear Achievement 18d, f)

✦ Sit in a circle and play music while the boys pass a mirror around. When the music stops, the boy holding the mirror looks at his reflection and tells one way that he is like Heavenly Father. (Wolf Elective 18c; Bear Achievement 18d, f)

✦ Read stories about princes or kings and talk about how each boy is the son of a heavenly king! Make crowns or decorate those paper ones from Burger King. (Wolf Elective 18c; Bear Achievement 18d, f)

✦ Read *The Velveteen Rabbit* and talk about the "real" worth of each boy. Learn how to sew fabric bunnies or some other rabbit craft. Do a Google search for "rabbit craft," and you'll find a lot of ideas to choose from! (Wolf Elective 3a, e; Wolf Elective 6b)

✦ Match baby animals to adult animals and see if the boys know what the babies are called. Talk about how they are like their Heavenly Father. Talk about the balance of nature in wildlife. (Webelos Naturalist 1a, b, c; 9; Academic Belt Loop for Wildlife Conservation)

✦ Have each boy sit in a chair and place a light behind his head. His profile will appear on the wall. Place a piece of poster paper on the wall and trace his profile. (Wolf Elective 3a, e)

✦ Talk with your Primary presidency to see if the boys could give talks on the subject "I Am a Child of God." You could also offer to do a sharing time presentation for the entire Primary. Check out the fun ideas listed under this topic at www.christysclipart.com/wwwroot/sharing_page.html (Webelos Communicator 2; Webelos Showman 1, 16)

✦ Paint and decorate clothespins to look like boys. Talk about how each one is unique and special, just like the boys. During the Christmas season, you could paint toy soldiers onto clothespins. (Webelos Artist 3, 6)

✦ Help the boys make goals to become a better person. (Wolf Achievement 11a, c; Wolf Achievement 12a; Bear Achievement 18a, c)

2

First Presidency Letter

Most every LDS Cub Scout can tell you who the current prophet is, but if you ask them who or what the First Presidency of the Church is, they might give you blank stares. Help them become familiar with the terminology of Church leadership and recognize the important mantle of authority. Help them feel a genuine love for the First Presidency and a desire to follow their guidance. Inspire them to follow the prophet their whole lives and teach them how they will be protected by their obedience.

✦ Read the First Presidency letter found in the front of the Faith in God pamphlet together and show pictures of who the current First Presidency is. Talk about each of the men, sharing stories from their lives that can be found in the Ensign by doing a search at www.lds.org. Explain what a presidency is and how it works. Help the boys become more familiar with President Thomas S. Monson by visiting his website together at www.thomasmonson.org (Wolf Elective 22c)

✦ Put a blanket on the floor, munch on snacks and watch the video about President Thomas S. Monson at www.thomasmonson.org or watch a DVD of one of his talks at General Conference. There are several videos on YouTube that show when it was announced that he would be the next President of the Church. (Webelos who do searches on the Internet to learn more about the prophet fulfill Communicator 12)

✦ Write a letter to the First Presidency, thanking them for all they do for the children in the world (Wolf Elective 21b; Webelos Communicator 11). Send cards and letters to:

> The Church of Jesus Christ of Latter-day Saints
> Church Office Building
> First Presidency
> 50 E. North Temple, Salt Lake City, Utah 84150

✦ Sing "Follow The Prophet" and have the boys make up verses for some of the latter-day prophets. They could draw pictures or make masks to look like some of the prophets. A booklet for the song can be found online at www.library.lds.org in the 1997 February *Friend* magazine. (Wolf Elective 11d, f; Webelos Showman 1, 9; Academic Belt Loop for Communicating; Academic Belt Loop for Music)

✦ Use pictures of latter-day prophets and apostles and play "Concentration" so the boys can become more familiar with their faces. Some cards with all of the new apostles' pictures can be cut into flash cards for the game at http://lds.about.com. (Wolf Achievement 10g, Webelos Communicator 12, Academic Belt Loop for Music)

✦ Share with the boys what some of the prophets were like when they were young by reading stories from the book *Boys Who Became Prophets* by Lynda Cory Hardy. (Bear Achievement 1a)

✦ Teach the boys how to sing "We Thank Thee, O God, for a Prophet" (Hymns, no. 19) and coordinate a date when they could sing it in sacrament meeting or during sharing time. Your Primary chorister may have some creative ways to help the boys remember all of the words to the song. (Webelos who know how to play the song on an instrument fulfill requirements for Showman 1 and 8. Wolf Elective 11d, f; Webelos Showman 1, 9; Academic Belt Loop for Music)

✦ Assign each boy a different modern-day prophet or one from the scriptures.

Have him bring a picture and teach the others about him at your gathering. (Bear Achievement 1a; Webelos Communicator 1, 16)

✦ Teach the boys how to make some of the prophets' favorite recipes such as Joseph Fielding Smith's sherbet, Harold B. Lee's boiled raisin cake, Spencer W. Kimball's raspberry cheesecake, Ezra Taft Benson's lemon meringue pie, or Wilford Woodruff's cherry nut cake. Recipes for some of the prophets' favorite dishes can be found at www.geocities.com/olstk/Prophetsfavorites.pdf (Bear Achievement 1a, Bear Achievement 9a, b, f)

✦ Find out when the current prophet's birthday is and send him a special card that the boys make for him. President Thomas S. Monson's birthday is August 21, 1927. (Wolf Elective 21b; Bear Achievement 1a)

✦ Help the boys make a collage of all the apostles that could be hung in the Primary room for all of the children to enjoy. (Bear Achievement 1a; Webelos Artist 10)

3

My Baptismal Covenant

Take turns reading each line of "My Baptismal Covenant." Try some of the following ideas to help them gain a greater understanding and appreciation for the promises that were made on their baptismal day:

✦ Invite the missionaries to speak to the children about how they teach investigators and prepare them for baptism. Encourage the boys to share experiences of baptisms they attended. (Wolf Achievement 11a, c, d; Bear Achievement 1a, b)

✦ Help each boy create a baptism resource binder. Guide the boys as they do Internet searches at the Church's Gospel library at www.lds.org. You can type in "baptism" to search in the *Friend* magazine or even check lesson manuals for ideas. Print out stories and talks about baptism for the boys to keep in their binders and read at home with their families for family home evening. (Webelos Communicator 12)

✦ Talk about being physically and spiritually clean. Show the boys how to make their own bar of soap by following the simple directions on www.teachsoap.com (Wolf Achievement 3a, b, c; Bear Achievement 1a, b; Webelos Athlete 2, 3)

✦ Help your boys memorize "My Baptismal Covenant" by playing games that review and test their learning. One technique is to write it on a chalkboard and

Primarily for Cub Scouts

slowly erase one word at a time while they learn each line. (Wolf Achievement 11a, c; Bear Achievement 1a, b)

✦ Learn about different people in the scriptures who have been baptized. Study the experience of Alma and the people who were baptized at the Waters of Mormon (Mosiah 18). Make puppets, flannel figures, or visual aids so the boys can share the stories with their families during family home evening. (Wolf Elective 22c; Wolf Elective 3a, e; Bear Achievement 1a; Webelos Showman 1, 2, 3, 4, 5, 6, 7)

✦ Have the children share special feelings about their baptisms. Create baptism scrapbook pages if they haven't already. A free digital scrapbook just for LDS baptisms can be found at www.sugardoodle.net (Bear Elective 11a, b, c, d; Webelos Artist Badge 2)

✦ Make gifts and cards that the boys could give to other children who will be getting baptized soon such as white towels or socks, frames, bags, or journals. Some cute poems that could go with them can be found at http://www.theideadoor.com/Baptism.html (Wolf Achievement 11c, d; Wolf Elective 3a, e; Wolf Elective 9b, c; Wolf Elective 17c; Bear Achievement 1b)

✦ Get a list from your Primary presidency of the children who will be getting baptized in the next year and their birthdates. Plan to attend their baptisms together as a pack. Prepare folders with information, word games, baptism puzzles, and other material to help prepare children for baptism. Present the folders to the children who will be baptized within the next year. More ideas are listed under www.christysclipart.com (Wolf Achievement 11c, d; Wolf Elective 3a, e; Bear Achievement 1b)

✦ Create a slide show presentation that could be shown at a baptismal service between the baptism and confirmation. Record the children singing Primary songs while a slide show of Church pictures is playing. (Wolf Elective 11d, f; Webelos Showman 1, 9, 11)

MY BAPTISMAL COVENANT

+ Learn a song that the boys could sing at someone's baptism. If any of the boys play a musical instrument, try to incorporate those talents in your musical number. (Wolf Elective 11d, f; Webelos Showman 1, 8, 9, 11; Academic Belt Loop for Music)

+ Have the boys make family home evening packets that include a lesson about baptism, visual aids, refrigerator magnet, a recipe for refreshments, and suggested scripture verses to read and songs to sing. You can even purchase a pre-made packet from www.hatchpatchcreations.com (Wolf Achievement 11c, d; Wolf Elective 3a, e; Bear Achievement 1b)

+ Draw pictures about baptism that could be used as artwork displayed at a baptism or used on the written program. The boys could also color the baptism clip art pictures found at www.bookofmormonposters.com (Wolf Elective 3a, e; Wolf Elective 12a, b, d; Webelos Artist 3, 4, 9, 10; Academic Belt Loop for Art)

+ Clean the baptismal font together in preparation for your ward's next baptism. (Wolf Achievement 11c, d; Bear Achievement 1b; Webelos Handyman 1a, b, 11)

+ Prepare a special sharing time presentation for your Primary about the importance of baptism and the covenants that are made. Some great ideas can be found in the July 2005 *Friend* magazine. (Wolf Achievement 9a)

+ Teach the boys how to make bookmarks or door hangers for their bedrooms with the words from "My Baptismal Covenant." If you use glow-in-the-dark paint, they will be reminded of the words even after their bedroom lights are off! (Webelos Artist 3, 9; Academic Belt Loop for Art)

+ See pictures and learn where former prophets were baptized by reviewing the article "Our Prophets' Places of Baptism" in the August 1997 issue of the *Friend*. (Bear Achievement 1a)

Primarily for Cub Scouts

+ Watch "Baptism—A Promise to Follow Jesus" Primary Video Collection #53179. (Wolf Achievement 11a; Bear Achievement 1a)

+ Create an ornament or bookmark that has a picture of the Savior being baptized on one side and a picture of each boy standing in front of the baptismal font in your Church building. (Wolf Elective 3a, e)

+ Invite some Young Men to share their thoughts on the Aaronic priesthood, the importance of the sacrament, and how we renew our baptismal covenants each Sunday. Teach the boys how to bake bread; it could be used in your ward the next Sunday for the sacrament. (Wolf Achievement 11c, d; Bear Achievement 1b; Bear Achievement 9b)

+ Arrange to have one or more of the boys give a talk at someone's baptism. (Webelos Communicator pin 2; Webelos Showman 1, 16)

+ Have the boys write a card, inviting people to attend their baptism. (Bear Achievement 18d; Academic Belt Loop for Communicating)

4

Award Requirements

Basic Requirements

Pray daily to Heavenly Father

✦ Go to www.lds.about.com to learn about the history of the pretzel and how it relates to prayer. Teach the boys how to make homemade pretzels and taste them with different kinds of mustard. With all that twisting, you might as well throw in a lesson on knot tying! (Wolf Achievement 11c; Bear Achievement 1a, b; Webelos Badge Requirement 8 e; Webelos Communicator 1, 12; Academics Belt Loop for Computers)

✦ Make "Prayer Rocks." You can find several different poems online to go with them. Throw in a little lesson about other kinds of rocks, and your boys can pass off some of the requirements to earn the Academics Belt Loop for Geology! (Wolf Achievement 11a, c; Bear Achievement 1a, b; Webelos Badge Requirement 8e; Webelos Geologist 1, 2, 3, 4, 6, 7, 9)

✦ Draw a face on a square block of wood, and add yarn for hair. Teach the boys to remember the four steps of prayer by showing them the four sides of a square: Dear Heavenly, We Thank Thee, We Ask Thee, In the name of Jesus Christ. (Wolf Achievement 5e; Wolf Achievement 11a; Bear Achievement 1a, b; Webelos Badge Requirement 8e)

✦ Learn how to sing and conduct Primary songs about prayer. Teach them a song in sign language or another tongue. Your boys could lead the song during sharing time once they're ready to share their musical talents. (Wolf Achievement 11a, c, d; Wolf Elective 11d, e; Bear Achievement 1a, b; Webelos Badge Requirement 8e; Webelos Communicator 3, 4, 5, 10; Webelos Showman 1, 8, 9, 11, 13, 14; Academic Belt Loop for Language and Culture; Academic Belt Loop for Music)

✦ Have a PJ's party in a tent. "PJ's" stands for Prayer, Journal, Scriptures. You can even have a pillow fight tournament. Then talk about these three things they need to do before they go to sleep each night. (Wolf Elective 6b; Wolf Elective 9a; Webelos Badge Requirement 8e)

✦ Help the boys write a letter to Heavenly Father and talk about how prayer is like writing a letter to someone we know and love. You could even teach them calligraphy to make their letters look fancy. (Wolf Elective 21b; Webelos Badge Requirement 8e; Webelos Communicator 11; Academic Belt Loop for Communicating)

✦ Talk about how music is a prayer unto God. Read Doctrine and Covenants 25:12. Invite the boys to bring and play their musical instruments. (Wolf Elective 11e; Webelos Badge Requirement 8e; Webelos Showman 1, 8, 11, 13, 14; Academic Belt Loop for Music)

✦ Teach the boys how to make rag rugs with strips of cloth that they can put on the floor next to their bed to remind them to pray. Check out http://www.netw.com/~rafter4/article.htm. You can also make prayer rugs by stenciling designs or words on free carpet store samples with fabric paint. (Wolf Elective 12e; Webelos Badge Requirement 8e; Webelos Artist 3)

✦ Talk about the importance of prayer and share stories about people who had their prayers answered. (Wolf Elective 22c; Webelos Badge Requirement 8e)

✦ Study the Lord's prayer found in Matthew 6:9–13. (Wolf Achievement 11a; Bear Achievement 1a, b; Webelos Badge Requirement 8e)

✦ Have the boys make up a secret language for their den and talk about different ways we can communicate. Talk about the proper language of prayer. (Wolf Achievement 7a; Webelos Communicator 3, 4, 5)

✦ Using clay, help the boys create a sculpture of a boy praying. (Wolf Elective 3a, e; Webelos Artist 7)

✦ Present each boy with his very own Prayer Bear. Oriental Trading Company is great for inexpensive gifts. Before ordering on-line, do a Google search for "coupon code" for the store, and you can save on shipping or a percentage off your order. You can also order by phone at 1-800-875-8480 or 1-800-228-2269. Include this poem:

> I'm just a little Prayer Bear,
> I'll sit upon your bed.
> It's my job to remind you
> When your prayers should be said.
> When you put me on your pillow
> As you make your bed each day,
> Remember as you hold me,
> To take the time to pray.
> Then when you go to bed at night
> And put me on the floor,
> Remember to take the time to kneel
> And say your prayers once more.

✦ Make those old-fashioned tin can telephones with a string attached and see if the boys can hear each other when talking. Compare talking on a phone to prayer. (Wolf 4a, c; Webelos Badge Requirement 8e)

✦ Give each boy a rope and tell him to make a knot without letting go of each end. They won't be able to do it (but it will be entertaining to watch them try!) Now, have them fold their arms like they're going to pray. Give each boy a rope again and tell him to pull each end. The knot will form easily! Talk about how,

PRIMARILY FOR CUB SCOUTS

with prayer, impossible tasks can be accomplished, and when life gets crazy, to hang on! Practice tying several knots, and teach the boys how to whip and fuse the ends of a rope. (Wolf Elective 17a, b, d, e, f, g; Webelos Badge Requirement 2 and 8 e; Webelos Outdoorsman 10; Arrow of Light 2)

✦ Show pictures of Joseph Smith Jr. in the Sacred Grove. Read James 1:5, and have the boys draw a picture or write down specific questions they'd like to ask Heavenly Father about. (Wolf Elective 12a, b, d)

✦ Decorate a gratitude journal where the boys could record the blessings they're grateful for. Challenge them to offer a prayer without asking for anything. (Webelos Badge Requirement 8e)

✦ Have each boy decorate a Popsicle stick with his name on it. Each time you open and close your den meeting or Activity Day, have the person saying the prayer choose a stick out of a container and include that person's name in his prayer. (Webelos Badge Requirement 8e)

✦ Make simple lion puppets, and share the story of Daniel in the lions' den. Make sound effects using household items. (Wolf Elective 2b, c, d, e; Webelos Showman 1, 2, 3, 4, 5, 6, 7)

✦ Bring pioneer items to share, and tell some of the stories of pioneers who had their prayers answered. This is a perfect idea to do during the month of July when we celebrate Pioneer Day. (Wolf Elective 2a, b, c, d)

✦ Arrange to have the boys give a talk about prayer during sharing time or at a den meeting. Some cute ideas are listed at www.sugardoodle.net. (Webelos Communicator 2)

✦ Show the boys how to find inspiring stories online about prayer at www.lds.org. (Webelos Communicator 12; Academic Belt Loop for Computers)

✦ Talk about how the boys could pray for courage to do what is right. There are some great scripture stories that illustrate courage and prayer and can be taught by using felt cutouts. For products or ideas on how to make your own cutouts, go to www.storytimefelts.com. (Bear Achievement 11g)

✦ Invite someone who is deaf to teach the boys about sign language and to show them how to pray using sign language. (Webelos Communicator 4, 9; Academic Belt Loop for Language and Culture)

Read the scriptures regularly

✦ Make bookmarks by laminating pressed flowers or attaching ribbons to a card each boy designs or to pictures of the Savior. (Wolf Elective 12a)

✦ Make sock puppets or marionettes that the boys could use to act out scripture stories. (Wolf Elective 2e; Webelos 1, 2, 3, 4, 5, 6, 7)

✦ Draw the head of a scripture character onto a piece of cardboard. Leave a hole in the middle for the boys' faces. Have the boys wear their "masks" and act out the story. (Wolf Elective 2a, d; Academic Belt Loop for Communicating)

✦ There are tons of fun recipes online for scripture cakes, cookies, and breads you could make so the boys can really sink their teeth into the scriptures! The ingredients are found within scripture verses. The classic "Scripture Cake" recipe can be found online at www.dltk-kids.com/recipes/old_scripture_cake.htm. (Bear Achievement 9b, f)

✦ Help the boys think harder about the scriptures in a fun way. Divide them into small teams and provide each group a set of scriptures and scripture reference clues that will direct them to various stores in your local mall. Meet at the food court for refreshments. A great sample can be found at http://www.lightplanet.com/mormons/ywc/activities/virtuous.htm. (Wolf Elective 18c)

✦ Find all of the scriptures that talk about light. Light candles outside, and take turns trying to extinguish them with squirt guns. Talk about how we can follow the Savior's light as well as reflect it. Show the boys how to make luminaries.

This would be a great activity to do around the holidays where lights are a predominant symbol. (Wolf Elective 3a, e)

✦ Make shrink art by cutting a piece of heavy plastic into the shape of objects or people in the scriptures. Draw on the plastic with permanent markers and punch a hole in one end of the shape so the design can be turned into a zipper pull for a backpack or a bookmark dangle. Lay the plastic on foil-covered sheets and heat in a warm oven until the designs shrink! (Wolf Elective 3a, e)

✦ Talk about various people in the scriptures who encountered rough water, such as Noah, Jonah, and Lehi's family. Create an obstacle course the boys have to ride on with a tricycle or on roller blades while the other boys shoot water at them with squirt guns. (Wolf Elective 18d; Wolf Elective 20b)

✦ Talk about how Christ invited the disciples to become "fishers of men" (Matthew 4:19). Have the boys learn how to fish or play one of those fishing carnival-type games. Invite the missionaries in your ward to join you and talk about what they do. (Wolf Elective 19a, b, c, d, e, f)

✦ Have the boys share their favorite scripture with one another and create a special wall hanging, bookmark, or door hanger with it. If you use glow-in-the-dark paint, the boys will be reminded to read the scriptures each night before they go to sleep! (Wolf Elective 22c; Webelos Artist 3)

✦ Decorate calendars at the beginning of a new year. Teach the boys how to create their own stickers that will remind them to read their scriptures each day. They have sticker-making machines at Walmart and Michaels, or else you can follow the simple directions found at www.essortment.com . (Wolf Elective 3a, e)

✦ Listen to inspiring music or a recorded Church talk while the boys mark their scriptures, using Seminary Scripture Mastery verses or the ones used in *Preach My Gospel*, or any others of their choosing. While listening, give each boy four pieces of long, skinny red licorice to see how many knots they can tie.

AWARD REQUIREMENTS

Two of the pieces are for knot tying while the other two are for eating. (Academic Belt Loop for Music)

✦ Help the boys make collages of their favorite scriptures in verse or picture. Hang them in the Primary room for all the children to see. (Wolf Elective 3a, e; Webelos Artist 10; Academic Belt Loop for Art)

✦ Draw a map of Church history sites, Book of Mormon lands, or Bible cities on a plastic tarp or tablecloth. Have the boys throw wet sponges on certain places as you read the scriptures mentioning them. Help the boys learn how to read a map and understand map legends and symbols. (Webelos who make a map of the United States fulfill requirements for Forester pin 1. Wolf Elective 4 f; Webelos Traveler 1, 9, 10; Academics Belt Loop for Map & Compass; Academics Belt Loop for Geography)

✦ Using clay, help the boys create a sculpture of the scriptures or of a person reading the scriptures. (Wolf Elective 3a, e; Webelos Artist 7; Academic pin for Art)

✦ Discuss the travels of famous missionaries in the scriptures (Paul, Alma the Younger, and the sons of Mosiah). Create a maze or obstacle course that follows their journeys. Draw a map that shows where your current ward or branch missionaries are serving. (Wolf Elective 18d; Bear Achievement 1a; Webelos Traveler 1, 10)

✦ Ask the boys to find a scripture about a particular topic or one that uses a specific word. When they do, they get to shoot a basket or throw a wadded up paper ball into a wastebasket. Top scorer wins. (Wolf Elective 20m)

✦ Choose one of the books in the Bible (or other scriptures) to be the clue for hangman. The boys can ask yes or no questions. Each time the answer is no, you draw another element on the hangman until they can guess the book. (Wolf 10g)

✦ Watch a video about a particular scripture story. There are tons of

Primarily for Cub Scouts

animated, dramatic, and even musical versions to be found in LDS and Christian bookstores! I love the ones at www.livingscriptures.com. (Wolf 10e)

✦ Show the boys how to access the online scripture database at www.lds.org. Have them do a search for a specific topic. (Webelos Communicator 12; Academic Belt Loop for Computers)

✦ Challenge the boys to write their own parable and share it with one another by acting it out or reading it. (Wolf Elective 2a; Webelos Communicator 8; Webelos Showman 1, 19; Academic Belt Loop for Communicating)

✦ Teach the boys how to bake bread and talk about the wise counsel: "Man shall not live by bread alone, but by every word that proceedeth out of the mouth of God." (Bear Achievement 9b)

✦ Decorate journals the boys could write in to record impressions they feel while reading the scriptures each night. (Wolf Elective 3a, e)

✦ Munch on goodies while listening to the scriptures on CD or cassette tapes. Even better, help the boys create their own recorded scripture drama! (Webelos 1, 19)

✦ Show the boys how to prepare "glue-ins" to put in their scriptures. A glue-in is a small picture with a quote from a prophet or apostle that adds insight to a particular scripture verse. The boys could design their own or you could try some of the free samples at www.kenalford.com. (Wolf Elective 3a, e)

✦ Bring a tape recorder and have the boys record their favorite scripture passages that could then be given to the elderly members in your ward who have trouble reading. (Wolf Achievement 11d; Bear Achievement 1b)

✦ Create illustrations to go with certain scripture stories. (Wolf Elective 3 a, e; Wolf Elective 12a, b, d)

✦ Take a field trip to your Church's library and you'll surely find some hidden gems: flannel board scripture stories, videos, "Scripture Readers," pictures, and tons more! (Wolf Elective 6a, b)

✦ Arrange to have one or more of the boys give a talk about the scriptures during sharing time or at a den meeting. (Webelos Communicator 2)

✦ Decorate the room with cars and traffic signs and theme the activity "Route 66." Talk about what's inside each of the sixty-six books in the Bible and how the scriptures are like a road map for our lives. Help the boys learn how to use a map and their symbols, timetables, and travel safety. You could even have the boys work on their Pinewood Derby cars! (Webelos 1, 2, 9, 10, 12; Academics Belt Loop Map and Compass; Academics Belt Loop Geography)

✦ Decorate little boxes of raisins to look like scriptures. Place black construction paper slightly over the edges of a gold-painted raisin box. Attach a little ribbon before you glue everything down and decorate the top to look like one of the Standard Works. (Wolf Elective 3a, e)

✦ Make scripture covers out of paper that the boys can color and decorate. (Wolf Elective 6c; Webelos Badge 8; Webleos Artist 4; Academic Belt Loop for Art)

Keep the commandments and live "My Gospel Standards"

✦ "My Gospel Standards" can be found in the boys' Faith in God booklet. It can also be found at http://www.lds.org/hf/art/display/1,16842,4218-1-6-174,00.html. Each of the boys could present one of the standards to the other boys and teach a mini lesson on it. (Webelos Showman 1, 16)

✦ Print out the free pdf file that includes cute clip art in a booklet about "My Gospel Standards." Each boy can color and create his own booklet to keep. To download the file, go to http://lds.about.com/od/visualmusicalaids/a/bk_gospelstand.htm. (Wolf Elective 3a, e; Webelos Badge Requirement 8e; Webelos Artist 4; Academic Belt Loop for Art)

PRIMARILY FOR CUB SCOUTS

✦ Decorate pillow cases by writing the "My Gospel Standards" theme with fabric ink. (Wolf Elective 3a, e)

✦ Learn how to cross-stitch by creating a wall hanging or pillow. Use the "My Gospel Standards" as the theme. (Wolf Elective 3a, e)

✦ Music is a great way to remember things. Tara Tarbet, a talented musician, has composed music for each of the standards. Children are better able to learn and internalize the gospel standards though songs. For free copies of the sheet music check out: http://www.mormonmomma.com/mini/gsmusic.html. (Wolf Elective 11d, e, f; Webelos Showman 1, 9; Academic Belt Loop for Music)

✦ Make door hangers with the "My Gospel Standards" written on them. (Wolf Elective 3a, e)

✦ Find another group of LDS boys in the world who would like to be pen pals. Share letters, pictures, and care packages. Talk about how the boys are living the commandments and "My Gospel Standards." Join an online discussion group (see websites chapter) to find Primary leaders who would be interested in forming such a pen pal friendship with your ward. (Wolf Elective 21b; Wolf Elective 22e)

✦ Have a fashion show, using newspaper and duct tape to make creative camping outfits and gear that the boys can wear down a mock runway. Award silly prizes for "Most Creative," "Most stylish," and so on. Talk about the importance of proper grooming and clothing for those who hold the priesthood. (Wolf Elective 3a, e)

✦ Talk about the courage to avoid peer pressure. You can find inexpensive CTR rings in any language at the Church Distribution Center. (Wolf Achievement 12; Webelos Readyman 1a, b, c; Academic Belt Loop in Language and Culture)

✦ Make puppets that the boys can dress in Sunday clothing and then do

AWARD REQUIREMENTS

various role-play scenarios such as passing the sacrament or collecting fast offerings. (Wolf Elective 2e; Wolf Elective 3a, e; Webelos 1, 2, 3, 4, 5, 6, 7)

✦ Make shrink art designs using gospel-oriented objects. Put a hole in the top so that a ribbon or rope could be threaded through and used to hang the shrink art to a backpack or scripture carrier. (Wolf Elective 3a, e)

✦ Make small "My Gospel Standards" cards that could be cut out and colored by the boys. Click on "Sharing Time" http://www.lds.org/churchmagazines/6-2006-Friend/Jun2006Friend.pdf. (Wolf Elective 3a, e)

✦ Invite "Moses" to attend your Activity Day so that your boys could interview him and learn about the Ten Commandments. This is a great opportunity for you to use the talents of your bishopric, ward missionaries, or dads! Bake sugar cookies into the shape of numbers and talk about each of the Ten Commandments. (Bear Achievement 9a)

✦ Decorate a poster or bulletin board in the Primary room to remind all of the children about "My Gospel Standards." (Wolf Elective 3a, e; Wolf Elective 12f; Academic Belt Loop for Communicating)

✦ Invite the missionaries to explain how they teach the commandments and standards of the Church to their investigators. (Wolf Achievement 11a, c, d; Bear Achievement 1a, b)

✦ Have the boys fill prescription bottles with candy and talk about how the gos-"PILL" is the best kind of medicine! Talk about the Savior as the Great Physician. (Wolf Achievement 11a, c; Wolf Elective 3a, e; Bear Achievement 1a)

✦ Talk about what faith is. (Wolf Achievement 11a, b, c; Bear Achievement 1a; Webelos Badge Requirement 8a, b, c, d, e)

✦ Invite the boys to make a list of things they can do to practice their religion. (Wolf Achievement 11c, d; Bear Achievement 1b)

✦ Help the boys make mobiles for their bedrooms, using thirteen elements to represent each line in "My Gospel Standards." (Wolf Elective 3a, e, Webelos Artist 8)

✦ Talk with your Primary presidency to see if the boys could give talks in sharing time about living the gospel and keeping the commandments. (Wolf Achievement 11c, d; Bear Achievement 1b; Webelos Communicator pin 2; Webelos 1, 16)

✦ Have the boys make and decorate bookmarks with the words from "My Gospel Standards." Examples can be found at http://theideadoor.com/Primary/GospelStandards.html. (Wolf Elective 3a, e)

✦ Shape Kool-Aid play dough into gospel-oriented designs:

>3 cups flour
>½ cup salt
>2 Kool-Aid packages
>2 cups boiling water

Mix dry ingredients together and then add boiling water. Knead on a floured board and then play! (Wolf Elective 3a, e)

Honor your parents and be kind to your family

✦ Bake cookies together that the boys can take home to their families. Encourage the boys to talk about the good things about their families. (Bear Achievement 9a; Webelos Family Member 1)

✦ Have the boys make candy-gram messages for their families. Help the boys think of messages to write where candy can take the place of words, such as "You are such a SMARTIE," "BeTWIXt you and me, I think our family is worth a HUNDRED GRAND." (Wolf Elective 3a, e; Webelos Family Member 1)

✦ Invite the boys to bring different kinds of stickers and stationery to write thank-you notes to their families. Show the boys how to make their own stickers by printing pictures on Avery sticker paper. You can also create a sticky backing on regular paper by brushing a gelatin mixture to the back. Follow the easy instructions at www.parenthood.com. (Wolf Elective 3a, e; Webelos Communicator 3, 4; Webelos Family Member 1)

✦ Help the boys decorate "Kindness Cans" to share with their families. Each time someone sees a family member do something kind, he or she writes it down on a slip of paper to put in the can. Read the slips of paper at the next family home evening. Talk about how the boys CAN be kind. (Wolf Achievement 10a; Wolf Elective 3a, e; Webelos Family Member 1)

✦ Have the boys make decorative gift bags from lunch bags. Fill with treats and have the boys present one to each member of his family with a note that says, "Having you in my family is sweet!" (Wolf Elective 3a, e; Webelos Family Member 1)

✦ Teach the boys how to make and decorate gingerbread houses during the holidays. Talk about what they can do to make their real homes sweeter. (Wolf Elective 3e; Webelos Family Member 1)

✦ Make sticky buns and have the boys take some home with a note that says "A loving family STICKS together!" (Bear Achievement 9a, f; Webelos Family Member 1)

✦ Celebrate "Respect for Parents Day" on August 1. Check out some fun craft ideas at www.dltk-holidays.com. Help the boys plan a fun night for their families. (Wolf 7a; Wolf Elective 3a; Webelos Family Member 1, 8)

✦ Make some kind of a family home evening task chart or board the boys can use each week at home to remember who is in charge of the lesson, prayer, refreshments, and so on. You can download some free charts at http://lds.about.com. (Wolf Achievement 10a; Wolf Elective 3e; Webelos Family Member 1, 2, 5, 8)

✦ Read *The Jungle Book* by Rudyard Kipling or watch one of the movie versions of the book and talk about the role of Akela in Cub Scouts. The front of

Primarily for Cub Scouts

each of the Cub Scout books includes parts of the story. Any adult leader in Cub Scouts is considered to be "Akela" and can pass off requirements to give the boys credit. Help the boys understand the importance of showing respect to their parents, leaders, teachers, and others who play the role of Akela in their lives. (Wolf Achievement 7a; Webelos Family Member 1)

✦ Help the boys draw a profile picture of a family member. Watch the online tutorial together at www.drawingnow.com. (Webelos Artist 6; Webelos Family Member 1)

✦ Teach the boys how to frame a nice copy of the "The Family: A Proclamation to the World" that they can hang in their bedrooms or homes. They could even make their own frame out of wood. A cute "Family Proclamation Cookie" recipe and story can be found at www.sugardoodle.net. (Wolf Achievement 11a, b, c; Webelos Craftsman pin 1, 2, 3; Webelos Family Member pin 1)

✦ Talk about fun family traditions. Invite each boy to share with the group some of the things his family does. Share some new ideas with them at www.foreverfamilies.com. (Wolf Achievement 10a, Bear Achievement 18f, Webelos Family Member 1)

✦ Using cardboard boxes, create "houses" and display a picture of each person in the family in a different window. Fill the box with goodies the boys can share with their families. (Wolf Elective 3 e; Webelos Family Member 1)

✦ Choose a nice location or backdrop and invite the families to have their pictures taken by someone in your ward with some photography talent. This could also be a great fundraiser for your pack. (Webelos Family Member 1, 8)

✦ Teach the boys how to do laundry correctly so that they can help their families at home with this chore. Do experiments to see which products work the best. (Webelos Family Member 1, 10)

✦ Help the boys create a coat of arms for their family to display by designing their own or searching for their historic coat of arms. See www.yourchildlearns.

com/heraldry.thm. (Wolf Elective 3 a, e; Webelos Family Member 1; Webelos Heritages belt loop)

✦ Visit your closest Family History Center to learn more about genealogy. Your ward or stake should have a consultant who can show you around and help teach the boys some basics. Encourage each boy to bring the name of one relative whom they can research. (Wolf Achievement 6b; Bear Achievement 8d; Webelos Family Member 1; Heritages Belt Loop)

✦ Help the boys print family trees that display their pedigree in a beautiful way. You can make your own or even buy one online where you get to choose from a variety of frames, styles, sizes, backgrounds, and fancy paper. Check out www.generationmaps.com. (Webelos Artist 3; Webelos Craftsman 1, 2, 3; Webelos Family Member 1)

✦ Create Christmas ornaments by using mini frames with family photos inside. You can also make ornaments out of quilted pieces of special fabric used for weddings or baby blankets. (Wolf Elective 3a, e; Webelos Family Member 1)

✦ Decoupage boxes, benches, stools, or even dressers by using copies of special photographs, drawings, or other cutouts that have special meaning to the family's history. (Wolf Electives 3a, e; Webelos Family Member 1; Webelos Handyman 12)

✦ Help the boys think of ways they can show kindness to their family members by giving compassionate service. See chapter 7, which lists tons of ideas for service projects. (Bear Achievement 24f; Webelos Badge Requirement 8e; Webelos Citizen 8; Webelos Family Member 1)

✦ Help the boys prepare a loving gift for a family member. See Chapter 8 for a list of arts and crafts ideas that fulfill Scout requirements. (Wolf Elective 3a, e; Bear Achievement 24f; Webelos Family Member 1; Academic Belt Loop for Art)

✦ Teach the boys how to prepare a meal for their families. If the meal is

PRIMARILY FOR CUB SCOUTS

prepared outdoors, then Webelos fulfill Outdoorsman 8. (Webelos Family Member pin 11; Webelos Fitness 3, 4)

✦ Build or create a special trunk where family history items can be stored. (Wolf Achievement 3a; Wolf Achievement 5a, b, c, d, e; Webelos Craftsman 1, 2, 4; Webelos Family Member 1; Webelos Handyman 12, 14, 15, 16, 17)

✦ Make quilts or pillows using family photos that have been transferred to fabric. (Wolf Elective 3a; Webelos Family Member 1)

✦ Help the boys design a calendar using family photos for each month. Include birthdates of important ancestors and other special family history events. (Wolf Elective 3a; Webelos Family Member 1; Academic Belt Loop for Heritages)

✦ Using copies of the boys' family photographs or drawings, design greeting cards. (Wolf Elective 3a, e; Webelos Family Member 1)

✦ Show the boys how to make their own diaries by using copies of pictures of ancestors to design the front cover and illustrate other pages throughout the book. (Wolf Elective 3a; Webelos Family Member 1; Academic Belt Loop for Heritages)

✦ Teach the boys the proper disposal of trash so they can help their families with this weekly chore. (Webelos Family Member 1; Webelos Naturalist 12)

✦ Using poster paper that comes on rolls, have the boys make a time line of their family's history. (Wolf Elective 3a; Webelos Family Member 1; Academic Belt Loop for Communicating)

✦ Discuss the importance of creating a positive attitude in your home and doing your part to make it happy. Talk about cooperation. There are some fun games that teach cooperation at www.youthwork-practice.com. (Wolf Achievement 10a; Webelos Family Member 1; Webelos Scholar 1a, b, c)

✦ Help the boys make a list of fun things they could do with their families. The boys can help create a special event just for families or work with the Scout Committee to plan a fun activity at your next pack meeting. (Wolf Achievement 10b, c, d, e, f, g; Bear Achievement 10b; Bear Achievement 12d, e; Bear Achievement 15a; Bear Achievement 17a, b; Bear Achievement 23d, e; Bear Elective 13c; Webelos Family Member 1, 5, 8)

✦ Ask your Primary presidency to arrange for your boys to give talks in sharing time or at a den meeting about honoring their parents. (Webelos Communicator 2; Webelos Family Member 1; Webelos Showman 1, 16)

✦ Talk to the boys about how they can encourage their family members and be supportive to one another. Have them write a loving letter to someone in their family who needs some extra kindness. (Bear Achievement 24d; Webelos Communicator 11, 13; Webelos Family Member 1)

✦ Talk to the boys about what respect means and how they can show it to their family members. For some creative ideas, go to www.rudebusters.com. (Bear Achievement 8g; Webelos Family Member pin 1)

✦ Plan a Cub Scout campout where the boys can go camping with their families. A perfect time to organize a father/son campout is in May to commemorate the restoration of the priesthood. If Boy Scouts will also be attending, then Webelos will fulfill requirements for Webelos Outdoorsman 4, 12. (Bear Achievement 12a; Webelos Family Member 1, 8; Webelos Outdoorsman 1, 2, 3, 5, 7, 8, 11)

✦ If the ward is holding an outdoor activity, you could include a family hike so that the boys could pass off Bear Achievement 12b. Work with your ward activity leaders to see how you can combine scouting and Primary goals with ward activities. Teach the boys the Outdoor Code. If your hike lasts for three miles, then Webelos can pass off the requirement for Outdoorsman 9. (Webelos Badge Requirement 7; Arrow of Light 5; Webelos Family Member 1, 5)

✦ Show each boy how to draw and laminate place mats for his family to use.

Primarily for Cub Scouts

Webelos who draw or paint an outdoor picture fulfill Webelos Artist Badge 3. (Wolf Elective 3a, e; Wolf Elective 12a, b, c, e; Webelos Family Member 1; Academic Belt Loop for Art)

✦ Decorate picture frames with buttons, silk flowers, or other small items for the boys to keep a family photo in, or some other picture they draw themselves. Even better, teach the boys how to cut wood to make their own frame. (Wolf Elective 3a; Webelos Artist 3; Webelos Craftsman 1, 2, 3; Webelos Family Member 1)

✦ Help the boys create their own Cub Scout scrapbook. Show them how to cut pictures and create interesting designs on each page. Remember to take pictures of the boys at each den and pack meeting for the boys to include in their scrapbooks. Include a picture of each boy's family. (Wolf Elective 3a; Bear Achievement 8f; Webelos Artist 2; Webelos Family Member 1)

✦ Using calligraphy, create a framed picture with each boy's family name and try to learn the historic meaning of that name. Check out www.last-names.net/Articles/Anatomy.asp. (Wolf Elective 3a, Webelos Artist 3; Webelos Craftsman 1, 2, 3; Webelos Family Member 1)

✦ Show the boys how to create a family party book where they write down all of the things their family does throughout the year to celebrate holidays, birthdays, anniversaries, baptisms, and any other special occasions. (Wolf Achievement 9b, c; Wolf Elective 3a, e; Webelos Communicator 8; Webelos Family Member 1, 5, 8)

✦ Invite each boy to find out his "culinary heritage" and bring a food dish to share with the others that represents his ancestors' home country. Help him create his own recipe book in a decorated binder. (Wolf Achievement 8c; Webelos Family Member pin 1; Academic Belt Loop for Heritages)

✦ Invite each boy's grandparents to a den meeting and celebrate Grandparents Day (the first Sunday after Labor Day). Some creative ideas for

AWARD REQUIREMENTS

activities and crafts they can do with their grandparents can be found at www.apples4theteacher.com and www.dltk-kids.com/crafts/grandparents/index.html. (Wolf Elective 3a, d, e; Webelos Family Member pin 1)

✦ Help the boys plan a menu for a picnic and have them invite their parents. (Bear Achievement 12c; Webelos Family Member pin 1, 8)

✦ Organize a fun family bike ride. The boys can decorate their bikes for a bike parade on Independence Day or Pioneer Day in July. Discuss bike safety and teach the boys how to lubricate their chains and inflate their tires. (Bear Achievement 14g; Webelos Athlete 8; Webelos Family Member 1, 8; Webelos Handyman 6, 7, 8; Webelos Readyman 9)

✦ Help the boys create funny anagrams, using the names of each member in their family to be shared at family home evening. A really great website that will find dozens of anagrams for you in seconds is http://wordsmith.org/anagram/. (Wolf Elective 1a; Webelos Family Member 1)

✦ Encourage the boys to take their families on a tour around their houses and talk about home safety. The boys could create a packet of material they could present at their next family home evening. (Bear Achievement 11e; Webelos Family Member 1, 6, 7; Webelos Fitness 2; Webelos Readyman 3, 11, 13)

✦ Provide paper and markers for the boys to write letters to family members who live far away. Take a photo of each boy to include in the letter. (Bear Achievement 18b; Bear 24d; Webelos Family Member 1)

✦ Help the boys begin keeping their own journals. Show them different kinds of journals, and have them decorate the outside of a book or binder they can use as their journal. Create a list of topics they can refer to when they can't think of anything to write. A sample can be found at www.thewritesource.com/topics.htm. (Bear Achievement 8f)

✦ Help the boys write a story about something they have done with their

PRIMARILY FOR CUB SCOUTS

family. (Bear Achievement 18f; Webelos Communicator 8; Webelos Family Member 1; Academic Belt Loop for Communicating)

✦ Discuss finances and how the boys can help their families save money. Help them design a sample family budget and create a family energy-saving plan. A sample is shown at www.personalbudgeting.com. (Webelos Family Member 1, 3, 4, 7)

✦ Talk to the boys about gratitude and help them write a thank-you letter to someone in their family. (Bear Achievement 24b, d; Webelos Communicator 11, 13; Webelos Family Member 1)

✦ Show the boys how they can search the Internet for ideas for their family home evening lessons. Help them plan a fun family night. (Webelos Communicator 12; Webelos Family Member 1, 5, 8)

✦ Help the boys make puppets that resemble each family member. (Wolf Elective 2e; Webelos Family Member 1; Webelos Showman 1, 2, 3, 4, 5, 6, 7)

✦ Help the boys make a creative chore chart for their families out of wood, felt, or paper. Show the boys how to properly vacuum or clean something by turning it into a relay. (Webelos Family Member 1, 2, 9, 10; Webelos Handyman 1a, b, 11)

Pay your tithing and attend tithing settlement

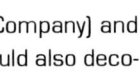

✦ Buy inexpensive piggy banks (Walmart or Oriental Trading Company) and have the boys decorate them while you talk about tithing. You could also decorate boxes or those round oatmeal containers to create piggy banks. (Wolf Elective 3a, e; Webelos Artist 9)

✦ Create special boxes with dividers for tithing, mission, education, savings, and spending money. Help the boys make the boxes look like cash registers. Talk about the importance of each area of money management. (Wolf Elective 3a, e; Academic Belt Loop for Mathematics)

- Talk about the importance of paying an honest tithe. Use candy pieces to show the boys how to figure out what a tenth is and tell them that paying tithing is sweet. (Bear Achievement 18h; Webelos Badge Requirement; Arrow of Light 7a, b, c)

- Teach the boys about Lorenzo Snow and the revelation on tithing. You might even find the Church movie entitled *The Windows of Heaven* in your ward library. (Wolf Elective 22c)

- Share uplifting stories about the blessings of tithing. (Wolf Elective 22c)

- Help the boys prepare a family home evening lesson about tithing that they can share with their families. Include stories with visual aids and a recipe for a dessert that could be cut into ten portions to further illustrate what ten percent is. Some sample ideas for lessons can be found at www.lds.about.com. (Wolf Elective 3a, e; Webelos Artist 9)

- Include a lesson on resourcefulness when talking about tithing and money. Have a contest to see who can clip the most coupons out of a newspaper the fastest. (Bear Achievement 21g; Academic Belt Loop for Mathematics)

- If you're lucky enough to live near a bishops' torehouse or family home storage center, take a field trip and talk about how tithes and fast offerings help the poor. Most canneries don't allow young children to operate the machinery, but the boys could help fold boxes and get a tour. (Webelos Traveler 1, 2, 3, 4, 5, 6, 9, 10)

- Encourage each boy's family to open a savings account for their Cub Scout so he can learn about saving money. You could go on a field trip to a friendly bank that offers special rewards for kids who save. (Bear Achievement 13b, c, d, e, f, g; Webelos Traveler 1, 2, 3, 4, 5, 6, 9, 10, 11; Academic Belt Loop for Mathematics)

- Arrange to have the boys give a talk in sharing time or at a den meeting about tithing. Help them prepare visual aids. (Webelos Communicator 2; Webelos Showman 1, 16)

PRIMARILY FOR CUB SCOUTS

Attend sacrament meetings and Primary regularly

✦ Help the boys decorate a special jar they can put a small item (marble, penny, candy, cotton ball) in to represent each time they attend their Church meetings. When the jar is full, the group can get a special treat. (Wolf Elective 3e; Webelos Artist 9)

✦ Help the boys prepare a "Sunday Bag" where they will keep their scriptures, pictures of Jesus, gospel coloring books, the *Friend* magazine, and other things they can quietly look at during sacrament meeting to help them be reverent. Using fabric paint, they could paint a canvas bag or backpack. A large collection of clip art and coloring pages can be found at www.jennysmith.net. (Wolf 3a, e; Webelos Artist 4, 9)

✦ Help each boy make a flipchart or picture book of the Savior that he could look at during sacrament meeting. (Wolf Elective 12a, b)

✦ Have the boys make a family home evening lesson with visual aids about the importance of the Sacrament and attending Church each week. Lesson ideas can be found at www.lds.about.com. (Wolf Elective 12a, b)

✦ Help the boys learn to tie a necktie to wear at church. (Wolf Elective 17f)

✦ Invite the boys to give a three-minute talk at a den meeting or in Primary about the importance of attending Church. (Webelos Communicator 2; Webelos Showman 1, 16)

✦ With the approval of your ward leaders, hold an outdoor sacrament meeting or other worship service. Appropriate occasions might include an Easter sunrise service or a special Christmas musical event on the temple grounds. Teach the boys the Outdoor Code. (Wolf Elective 23h; Webelos Badge Requirement 7)

Other Requirements

Write your testimony

✦ Play inspiring music while you allow time for the children to write their testimonies on pages 14 and 15 in their Faith in God pamphlet. (Wolf Achievement 11c; Webelos Communicator 8)

✦ Talk about what a testimony is and the proper way to share it during fast and testimony meeting at Church. Invite the boys to share their testimonies at your ward's next fast and testimony meeting. (Wolf Achievement 11a, b, c)

✦ Show the boys how to prepare a Book of Mormon to give to an investigator by marking key scriptures and writing their testimony in the front. Give books to the missionaries to use with their investigators, or challenge the boys to give them away to their friends. (Wolf Achievement 11c, d)

✦ Teach the boys how to do calligraphy and write their testimonies on beautiful paper. (Wolf Achievement 11c, Webelos Communicator 8)

✦ Create a "Primary Principles" binder where each boy gets an opportunity to write his feelings about the gospel. When the binder is complete it may be presented to the bishop, Cub Master or Primary president. (Wolf Achievement 11a, b, c, d; Webelos Communicator 8)

✦ Before each boy spends time writing his testimony, have him create something fun to write with. Using floral tape, wrap the stem of a silk flower or plastic figure to a pen or pencil. Put beans in a clay pot or decorated tin can to hold his pen. (Wolf Elective 3e, Wolf Elective 9b, c; Webelos Communicator 8)

✦ Have the boys talk about how a testimony is like a balloon (it requires effort, it grows a little bit at a time, it can puncture easily). Write on slips of paper things the boys can do to gain a testimony, such as prayer, studying the scriptures, obeying the commandments, attending Church, and so on. Put the slips of paper in balloons, and have the boys pop balloons by sitting on them. Let them read aloud what is written. (Wolf Achievement 11a, b, c)

✦ Share scriptures that teach about faith and how our testimonies can grow. Teach the boys about gardening, and have each boy plant a seed. Have the boys write one sentence of their testimony each week in a folder they decorate themselves, and see how their testimonies grow to fill each page. Talk about the "roots" of a testimony and how we can "experiment upon the word." Read Alma 32 together. (Wolf Achievement 11a, b, c; Wolf Elective 15c; Webelos Badge Requirement 8a, b, c, d, e)

✦ Involve the boys in making a board game and cards that reveal things that either help or hinder our testimonies. Have them create their own marker out of clay and then play the game by taking turns selecting cards and moving ahead or behind spaces until they reach the end (a strong testimony). (Wolf Achievement 11a, b, c)

✦ Teach the boys the hymn "Testimony" (no. 31) and arrange for them to sing it in Primary or sacrament meeting. Teach them how to read the musical notes and conduct the song as well. (Wolf Achievement 11a, b, c, d; Wolf Elective 11d, e, f; Webelos Showman 1, 9, 11, 13, 14; Academic Belt Loop for Music)

✦ Using building blocks, with a gospel principle written on each one, have the boys take turns selecting a block to stack to create a large structure. Invite them to share their feelings about why they chose their particular block and why its gospel principle is important to them. Be sure to include four blocks that say "Faith in Jesus Christ," "Repentance," "Baptism," and "The Gift of the Holy Ghost" to be the foundation of the building. Without even knowing it, they will be bearing their testimonies as they talk about the importance of each one! (Wolf Achievement 11a, b, c; Wolf Elective 3a, e; Webelos Badge Requirement 8a, b, c, d, e)

✦ Show the boys how to create a "Why I Believe" scrapbook journal, using photos, quotes, and written testimony. (Wolf Achievement 11a, b, c; Wolf Elective 3a, e; Webelos Artist 2)

AWARD REQUIREMENTS

+ Talk about what courage is. Share ideas of how to have enough courage to share our testimony at Church or with non-member friends. Invite the ward missionaries to share their experiences and then play fun games with them afterwards. (Wolf Achievement 12a; Webelos Readyman 1a, b, c)

+ Do a sand art project and compare the grains of sand to the faith-promoting experiences that when added upon one another, create a beautiful testimony. There is a fun online sand art game the boys could play at http://hicards.com/games/sand.html. (Wolf Achievement 11 a, b, c, Webelos Badge Requirement 8 a, b, c, d, e)

+ Build and paint a wooden box together that the boys can put their testimony-building items in: scriptures, journal, Faith in God booklet, handouts from Primary lessons, and so on. (Wolf Achievement 5a, b, c, d, e; Wolf Elective 3a, e; Webelos Badge Requirement 8a, b, c, d, e; Webelos Artist 3, 9; Webelos Craftsman 1, 2, 4; Webelos Handyman 12, 14, 15, 16, 17; Academic Belt Loop for Art)

+ Create a Sacred Grove experience for the boys by taking a hike out in nature. Set up stations that allow them to spend some quiet time alone with their scriptures and journal. Invite a speaker to talk about the Book of Mormon and how he or she gained a testimony of it. If the hike lasts for three miles, then Webelos fufill requirements for Outdoorsman 9. This could be a fun activity to include in the father/son campout in May to commemorate the restoration of the Aaronic priesthood. While out in nature, identify birds, plants, and animals. If older Boy Scouts attend the campout, then Webelos can fulfill Outdoorsman pin 4, 12. (Wolf Achievement 10c; Wolf Elective 18e; Webelos Naturalist Badge; Arrow of Light 5; Webelos who draw or paint an outdoor picture fulfill Webelos Artist Badge 3; Webelos Naturalist 1a, b, c, 5, 6, 7, 8, 9, 10; Webelos Outdoorsman 1, 2, 3, 7, 8, 11; Academic Belt Loop for Art; Academic Belt Loop for Wildlife Conservation)

+ Talk about how the Holy Ghost testifies of the truth and help the boys to recognize its promptings. Emphasize that it can speak to us in different ways: through our mind, heart, and spirit. Read scriptures that identify the fruits of the spirit (Galatians 5:22). Taste different kinds of exotic and unusual fruit the boys may have never seen before. (Wolf Achievement 11a, b, c)

✦ Teach the boys this new song about testimonies at www.songsoftheheart.com/ltestimony.html. Teach them how to read the notes and conduct in 2/4, 3/4, and 4/4 time. (Wolf Achievement 11a, b; Webelos Showman 1, 9, 11, 13, 14; Academic Belt Loop for Music)

Memorize the Articles of Faith and explain what they mean

✦ Teach the children different memorizing techniques to help them learn the Articles of Faith on page 16 of their Faith in God booklets. One simple method is to write the words on a chalkboard and remove one word at a time until the boys can remember the whole sentence without any visual clues. (Wolf Achievement 11a, b, c; Bear Achievement 1a; Webelos Badge Requirement 8a, b, c, d, e)

✦ Create a chart together to keep track of which Articles of Faith the boys have passed off. You'll know at a glance which articles you need to spend time on as a group. Let them know that if they can learn all of the Articles of Faith now, then it'll be a piece of cake when they need to pass them off again as Deacons for the Duty to God award. Eat cake when they're finished! Helpful charts can be found at www.lds.about.com as well as www.theideadoor.com (Bear 1b; Webelos Artist 1)

✦ Every time a boy passes off an Article of Faith, give him a token. The tokens can then be exchanged for toppings at a pizza or ice cream sundae party. (Wolf Achievement 11a, b, c; Bear Achievement 1a; Webelos Badge Requirement 8a, b, c, d, e)

✦ Have the boys create a "cheat sheet" for each Article of Faith by writing only the first letter of each word. No need to reinvent the wheel; www.scriptorian.com already has created some for you. Play games by mixing up the cheat sheets to see if they can guess which Articles of Faith are which. (Wolf Achievement 11a, b; Bear Achievement 1a)

AWARD REQUIREMENTS

♦ Create a small poster or door hanger that could be displayed in each boy's bedroom where all of the Articles of Faith are displayed as a reminder for him. There are some cute ideas at www.sugardoodle.net. (Wolf Achievement 12a, b, c, e, f; Bear Achievement 1a; Webelos Artist 9)

♦ Laminate the small Church cards that have the Articles of Faith on them to create bookmarks. Add a ribbon or beads to help mark the page. (Wolf Elective 3e; Bear Achievement 1a; Webelos Artist 9)

♦ Discuss what faith is. Act out scripture stories of people who showed great faith. (Wolf Achievement 11a, b, c, d; Webelos Showman 1, 19; Webelos Badge Requirement 8a, b, c, d, e)

♦ Talk about the importance of honesty and help the boys memorize Article of Faith 13, which says "We believe in being honest . . ." Have the boys draw a picture of Pinocchio and poke a wooden dowel or chopstick through his nose as you tell the story about how his nose grows when he lies. They could create a family home evening packet to take home and share with their families. (Bear Achievement 18h; Webelos Badge Requirement; Arrow of Light 7a, b, c)

♦ Help the boys make a list of ways they can help the Church during the week or month. A perfect project would be to sign up to clean the building. (Wolf Achievement 11d; Bear Achievement 11a; Webelos Badge Requirement 8a, b, c, d, e; Webelos Handyman 1a, b, 11)

♦ Have each boy choose an Article of Faith to write a poem about. Take turns reading the poems and guessing which Article of Faith it applies to. (Webelos Badge Requirement 8a, b, c, d, e)

♦ Have each boy choose an Article of Faith to draw a picture clue about and then see if the others can guess which Article of Faith it applies to. Display the pictures each time you review the Articles of Faith with the boys. (Wolf Achievement 11a, b, c; Wolf Elective 12a; Bear Achievement 1a; Webelos Badge Requirement 8a, b, c, d, e)

♦ Have the boys make a mobile, writing each Article of Faith on a different element to be hung, such as on stars or other themed shapes. (Wolf Achievement 11a, b, c; Wolf Elective 3e; Webelos Badge Requirement 8a, b, c, d, e; Webelos Artist 8)

♦ While the boys practice reciting the various Articles of Faith, have them make ice cream by turning the crank on a homemade ice cream maker. Check out the fun recipe for "Soup-Can Ice Cream" in the July 1987 issue of the *Friend* or ice cream in a bag at http://crafts.kaboose.com/ice-cream-in-a-bag.html. (Wolf Achievement 11a, b, c; Bear Achievement 1a; Webelos Badge Requirement 8a, b, c, d, e)

♦ Give the boys a bead, shell, or other small item to go on a key ring for every Article of Faith memorized. The boys could learn how to make one of those famous Scout lanyard key chains! (Wolf Achievement 11a, b, c; Bear Achievement 1a; Webelos Badge Requirement 8a, b, c, d, e)

♦ Do crossword puzzles that can be found online for each Article of Faith. You can even have the boys design their own at www.puzzle-maker.com or www.armoredpenguin.com/crossword/. (Wolf Achievement 11a, b, c; Bear Achievement 1a; Webelos Communicator 3, 12; Academic Belt Loop for Computers)

♦ Create a carnival atmosphere where the boys visit booths representing each Article of Faith. They can play games and win prizes each time they pass one off. (Wolf Achievement 11a, b, c; Wolf Elective 4a, b, c, d; Bear Achievement 1a; Webelos Badge Requirement 8a, b, c, d, e)

♦ Spray paint old keys gold, and present one to each boy after he passes off an Article of Faith. By the time he graduates from Primary he should have earned the "Thirteen Keys to the Kingdom." Talk about the importance of priesthood keys. Show the boys how to make a lanyard for their keychain. (Wolf Achievement 11a, b, c; Bear Achievement 1a; Webelos Badge Requirement 8a, b, c, d, e)

AWARD REQUIREMENTS

♦ Learn the Primary songs that go with each Article of Faith. The Primary Songbook can be downloaded for free at www.lds.org. (Wolf Achievement 11a, b, c; Wolf Elective 11d, e, f; Bear Achievement 1a; Webelos Badge Requirement 8a, b, c, d, e; Webelos Showman 1, 9, 11; Academic Belt Loop for Music)

♦ Invite a native speaker of another language or a returned missionary to say one or more of the Articles of Faith in another language. Help the boys learn how to say a few words. (Wolf Achievement 22a, b; Webelos Communicator 4, 10; Academic Belt Loop in Language and Culture)

♦ Have a friendly competition with the Activity Day girls to see who can memorize all thirteen Articles of Faith first. The winners receive a treat from the others. (Wolf Achievement 11a, b, c, d; Bear Achievement 1a; Webelos Badge Requirement 8a, b, c, d ,e)

♦ Create a Jeopardy game using words and clues from each of the Articles of Faith. A helpful sample is at www.sugardoodle.net. (Wolf Achievement 11a, b, c; Bear 1a)

♦ Teach the contents of the Articles of Faith using an ABC game found at www.theideadoor.com. (Wolf Achievement a, b, c; Bear Achievement 1a; Webelos Badge Requirement 8a, b, c, d, e)

♦ Ask your Primary presidency if your boys could give talks in sharing time about some of the Articles of Faith. (Webelos Communicator 2; Webelos Showman 1, 16)

♦ Go online together to test the boys' knowledge on the Articles of Faith at http://lds.about.com/library/bl/primary/blarticlestest.htm. (Wolf Achievement 11a, b, c; Bear Achievement 1a; Webelos Badge Requirement 8a, b, c, d, e; Webelos Communicator 12; Academic Belt loop for Computers)

♦ Have the boys make a list of things they can do during the week to practice their religion. (Wolf Achievement 11c, d)

PRIMARILY FOR CUB SCOUTS

Complete activities in the guidebook for the 4 areas on pages 6–12

Use the ideas in the next few chapters to get your own creative juices flowing. Brainstorm with the boys for fun things they'd like to do that allow them to accomplish their goals. You could write all of the activity goals on slips of paper and have the boys pick one out of a hat each time you're together to decide which one you'll do next.

✦ Create posters or decorative charts the boys could use to keep track of the progress on their goals if they'd like to use something in addition to the form on page 20 of their booklets. (Wolf Elective 3a, e; Wolf Elective 12f; Webelos Artist 9; Academic Belt Loop for Art; Academic Belt Loop for Communicating)

✦ Put together a calendar with the boys that shows when they need to pass off certain requirements and coordinates holidays and other events that fit nicely with the activities. (Wolf Elective 12f)

✦ Help the boys schedule an interview with a member of your bishopric or branch presidency.

✦ Play games with the members of your bishopric or branch presidency so the boys get to know them better and begin to fill comfortable with them. (Wolf Elective 4a, b, c, d, e, f; Wolf Elective 20a, j, k, l, m, o)

✦ Play games with the other boys while each one has a turn to be interviewed and discuss his Faith in God progress with a member of your bishopric. (Wolf Elective 4a, b, c, d, e, f; Wolf Elective 20a, j, k, l, m, o)

✦ To help the boys better appreciate the leaders of their ward, decorate the outside of the bishopric's door at Church with kind notes, photographs, and drawings, thanking them for their service to the ward. (Wolf Achievement 11d)

✦ Prepare treats for the bishopric to munch on during those long Sundays in December when they are busy doing tithing settlements with families. (Wolf Achievement 11d)

✦ With the approval of the Primary presidency, invite the bishopric to join the Primary during sharing time on Sunday. Sing some special songs you've been preparing for them. (Wolf Elective 11d, f; Webelos Showman 1, 9, 11; Academic Belt Loop for Music)

✦ Create a gift to present to the bishop on Father's Day for being such a good "Father" to the ward. (Wolf Elective 9b, c)

✦ Bake cookies and deliver them to the families of the bishopric. (Wolf Achievement 11d)

✦ Role-play an interview with the bishop so the boys will know what to expect. (Webelos Showman 2, 5, 19)

5

Learning and Living the Gospel

More important than simply learning the gospel is living it and loving it! Your Cub Scouts see you in a Church setting on Sunday, where everyone is dressed nicely with big smiles, but when you get together for den and pack meetings, they'll see you in more of a "real" setting. Do you practice what you preach? Do you show them how to live the gospel with joy? Here are some ideas to help them learn about the gospel of Jesus Christ and then to choose to live it! Practice makes perfect!

✦ A fun gospel craft is to decoupage words on strips of paper to clear stones or flat, clear marbles so the words show through. Word strips could include gospel principles, Articles of Faith, scriptures, "My Gospel Standards," or simply the boys' names. You could even teach the boys how to make little drawstring bags out of leather to keep their stones in or glue a magnet on the bottom so the stones could hang on their refrigerator at home. This would be a perfect time to go through requirements for the Webelos Geologist pin and/or the Geology Belt Loop. Share the Book of Mormon story about the Brother of Jared and when the Lord touches his stones to create light for the barges (Ether 3). (Wolf Elective 3e)

✦ Sit on pillows and munch on snacks while listening to a podcast of BYU devotionals, General Conference, or LDS music at www.apple.com/itunes/. (Wolf Achievement 11a, b, c; Academic Belt Loop for Music)

- Play "Stump the Bishop." Have the boys bring miscellaneous items from home that are placed in a special box or bag. The "Stumpee" has to pull each item out and then explain how it relates to gospel principles. The boys could also do this with each other. You'll be impressed how creative they can be! (Wolf Achievement 11a, b, c)

- Help the boys visit www.mormon.org to see all the great things there are for them to learn and share with their non-member friends. (Wolf Achievement 11a, b, c; Webelos Communicator 12)

- Gather small items of things that are mentioned in the scriptures to create "I Spy" pouches. Place items inside a Ziploc baggie and fill with colored beads. These make great quiet time entertainment for little ones during sacrament meeting or in the nursery, as long as the bags are sealed tightly and the contents can't come out. (Wolf Elective 3a, e)

- Play "Ask the Scriptures." Have the boys write questions on slips of paper that will be put into a box. Have a speaker come who will select a question one at a time to answer. The boys could also take turns individually or in groups finding the answers. They might be more willing to ask more honest questions if they know their identity will be anonymous. (Wolf Achievement 11a, b, c)

- Teach the boys how to make beanbags. Toss a beanbag to one of the boys, asking him a gospel-related question. Once he answers the question, he tosses the beanbag to someone else and asks the next boy a question. Continue until everyone has had a turn. (Wolf Achievement 11a, b, c)

- Help the boys review Cub Scouting's 12 Core Values, which are listed in their scout books under "Character Connections" and relate them to gospel principles. Play a matching game to see if they can match the values to all of the Articles of Faith. For example, the Responsibility Core Value could go with Articles of Faith numbers 2, 3, and 4. (Wolf Achievement 11a, b, c; Webelos Badge Requirement 8a, b, c, d, e)

Primarily for Cub Scouts

♦ Have the boys sing karaoke to Primary songs! Webelos who discuss opera and musicals also pass off Showman 22. (Wolf Elective 11d, e, f; Webelos Showman 1, 9, 11; Academic Belt Loop for Music)

♦ Teach the boys about food storage. Sample different recipes using classic food storage ingredients such as wheat, oats, and dried milk. There are tons of food storage recipes online at www.beprepared.com, www.waltonfeed.com, and www.mormonchic.com. (Wolf Elective 16a, b)

♦ Cut different lengths of pipe to create musical chimes. Learn how to play some Primary songs with them that could be performed in sacrament meeting or sharing time. You can find measurements and instructions online at www.familyfun.com. (Wolf Elective 3e; Wolf Elective 11d, f; Webelos Showman 1, 8, 11, 13, 14; Academic Belt Loop for Music)

♦ Build gingerbread houses together during the holiday season and talk about the "sweet" gospel principles that we can "build" our lives and testimonies on. (Wolf Achievement 11a, b, c; Wolf Elective 3e)

♦ Using masking tape, create a giant tic-tac-toe board on the floor. Ask scripture questions to review gospel principles. Players can place giant X's and O's, or use team members to stand on the square of their choice after correctly answering each question. (Wolf Achievement 11a, b, c)

♦ Have each boy choose several gospel terms and scramble the letters. The others will guess what the word is. Discuss the term for a few minutes before moving on to another one. (Wolf Achievement 11a, b, c)

♦ Set up a tour of your local Family Home Storage Center and teach the boys about self-reliance and the Church's welfare program. (Wolf Achievement 9a; Wolf Achievement 10a; Wolf Elective 16b)

♦ Play the CTR trivia game found at http://www.mormonshare.com/node/6673. (Wolf Achievement 11 a, b, c)

♦ Teach the boys how to make candles, and talk about what it means to "wax strong" in the gospel. There are tons of recipes and styles to choose from online. (Wolf Achievement 11a, b, c; Wolf Elective 3e)

♦ Tweak some of the popular TV game show ideas to help the boys learn and review gospel principles. Shows that work well are *Jeopardy*, *Password*, *Hollywood Squares*, and *Who Wants to be a Millionaire*. Play music from the show and make "Cub Scout Cash" or "Cub Coins" they can earn to spend on various prizes. (Wolf Achievement 11a, b, c)

♦ Teach the boys how to make flannel board stories by gluing fabric to the back of pictures. They can tell stories from the scriptures or Church history. The pictures can be given to your ward library or used for each boy's family home evening. (Wolf Achievement 11d; Wolf Elective 12a)

♦ Talk about the importance of character, respect, and attitude. Show clips from famous movies that demonstrate those traits. This is a perfect time to pass off requirements on the "Character Connections" in the boys' handbooks. (Wolf Achievement 6a; Wolf Achievement 7a; Webelos Scholar 1a, b, c)

♦ Using a big roll of paper, create a board game that teaches and tests the boys' gospel knowledge. Let them create their own rules and design. You can tweak an already popular game like "Chutes and Ladders" or "Mormonopoly." Invite the boys to create their own game pieces out of clay. Teach the boys how to put pictures of their faces on "Cub Cash" dollars (instead of the Presidents' faces). (Wolf Achievement 11a, b, c; Wolf Elective 12a)

♦ Invite each boy to bring a different kind of fruit. Teach them how to make smoothies and talk about the importance of good nutrition and the Word of Wisdom. Ask them what the "fruits" of the Spirit are and read Galatians 5:22. (Wolf Achievement 8a; Webelos Fitness 1, 5, 6, 7, 8)

♦ A fun gospel "Cranium" game can be found at www.sugardoodle.net/Primary/Primary%20Cranium.pdf. (Wolf Achievement 11a, b, c)

Primarily for Cub Scouts

✦ Check out http://abacuspc.hypermart.net/sem/ for some fun gospel-oriented board games. (Wolf 11abc)

✦ Play a game where the boys have to create scenarios that demonstrate choices they have to make in their lives. The boys act out the problem and then what the right thing to do is. (Wolf Achievement 12b, c, d, e, f, g, h, i, j, k; Bear Achievement 24e)

✦ Teach the boys about emergency preparedness and help them create a 72-hour kit in a can, backpack, or bucket. There's even a clever idea online for using an old sweatshirt for a kit at www.bevscountrycottage.com . (Wolf Elective 16a, b, c)

✦ Go on a field trip to the grocery store and have the boys read food labels to determine which foods are in keeping with the Word of Wisdom. (Bear Achievement 13a; Webelos Fitness 1, 5, 6, 7, 8; Webelos Traveler 2, 3, 4, 5, 6, 7, 11; Academics Belt Loop Map & Compass)

✦ Ask the boys to give a three-minute talk at a den meeting or sharing time about the joys and blessings of living the gospel. (Webelos Communicator 2; Webelos Showman 1, 16)

✦ Read James 1:27, and talk about what pure religion is. Describe compassion, and make a list of service the boys could do to help others. Chapter 7 includes several ideas for service projects. (Bear Achievement 24f; Webelos Badge Requirement 8e; Webelos Citizen 8, 17)

IDEAS FROM THE FAITH IN GOD BOOKLET:

Learning and Living the Gospel: (Complete at least two of the following activities each year)

✦ Explain how taking the sacrament helps you renew your baptismal covenant. In a family home evening, teach others about things we can do to remain faithful. (Wolf 11; Bear 1; Webelo Badge 8; Webelo Family Member 5)

✦ Give a family home evening lesson on Joseph's Smith First Vision (see Joseph Smith—History 1:1–20). Discuss how Heavenly Father answers our sincere prayers . (Wolf 11; Wolf Elective 22c; Bear 1a; Webelo Family Member 5; Religious Knot patch)

✦ Mark these verses about the Holy Ghost in your scriptures: John 14:16–17, 2 Nephi 32:5, and Moroni 10:5. Discuss ways the Holy Ghost helps you. (Wolf 11; Webelos badge 8e)

✦ Read a recent conference address given by the prophet. Decide what you can do to follow the prophet, and do it. (Wolf 11; Bear 1b, 18a; Webelos Badge 8e)

✦ Give an opening and a closing prayer in family home evening or at Primary. Share your feelings about how prayer protects us and helps us to stay close to Heavenly Father and the Savior. (Wolf 11; Bear 1; Webelos Family Member 5; Religious Knot patch)

✦ Tell a story from the Book of Mormon that teaches about faith in Jesus Christ. Share your testimony of the Savior. (Wolf 11a; Wolf Arrow 22c; Bear 1a; Webelos Badge 8a; Religious Square Knot patch)

✦ Read Doctrine and Covenants 89. Discuss how Heavenly Father blesses us when we faithfully live the Word of Wisdom. Help plan and conduct an activity to teach the Word of Wisdom to others. (Wolf 3a; 12b; Bear 9d; Webelos Communicator 2; Webelos Fitness 4,5,6,7,8)

✦ Prepare a pedigree chart with your name and your parents' and grandparents' names. Prepare a family group record for your family and share a family story. Discuss how performing temple work blesses families. (Wolf 11; Bear 8d; 18f; Webelos Family Member 12; Religious Knot patch)

✦ Learn to sing "Choose the Right" (Hymns, no. 239). Explain what agency is and what it means to be responsible for your choices. Discuss how making good choices has helped you develop greater faith. (Wolf 9a 12; Wolf Elective 11d, e; Bear 1b, 24e; Webelos Handyman 1)

6

Serving Others

The Cub Scout goal is to "Do a Good Turn Daily." Review the Cub Scout Promise and talk about ways the boys can help other people. Choose a few of the boys' ideas and incorporate them into your calendar of events. Also review the "Law of the Pack," and have the boys create a list of specific things they can do in the upcoming month to demonstrate how "the Cub Scout gives goodwill." If your den or pack plans to do a service project that benefits the environment, then your boys will fulfill some of the requirements for the World Conservation Award, "Leave No Trace" Awareness Award, and the Webelos Badge.

Some terrific resources with information on service organizations and projects the boys could get involved with are: www.volunteermatch.org, www.serviceleader.org, and www.servenet.org. You'll find some more great ideas at www.theideadoor.com. (All activities below fulfill Webelos Badge Requirement 8e; Webelos Citizen pin 8; and the Academic Belt Loop for Citizens!)

✦ Learn to crochet squares for the Red Cross "Warm Up America" Program. They collect squares from volunteers and then create blankets out of them for the needy. For information call (704) 824-7838 or go to www.warmupamerica.org.

✦ Celebrate "Be an Angel" Day on August 22 by doing a service project and making an angel craft. Fun ideas can be found at http://www.dltk-bible.com/paper-angels.html (Wolf E 3a, e; Webelos Artist 9)

✦ Hold a car wash but don't charge for the service. Give patrons a missionary pass-along card, and let them know you are there to serve the community.

✦ Organize a book drive for your local Boys & Girls Club, hospitals, library, or homeless shelters.

✦ Volunteer at the Salvation Army, Deseret Industries, or a local food bank.

✦ Check out www.allcrafts4charity.org and www.bevscountrycottage.com to learn about projects the boys can make and donate. (Wolf Elective 3a, e)

✦ For outdoor service projects sponsored by the Keep America Beautiful Foundation go to www.kab.org. When your boys become Boy Scouts they can earn the "Hometown USA" award by doing environment-friendly service projects. Teach the boys the Outdoor Code. (Bear Achievement 6g; Webelos Badge Requirement 7; "Leave No Trace" Awareness Award; World Conservation Award)

✦ Teach the boys how to knit projects like clothes for stuffed bears that are given to children in crisis by Precious Pals or Project Linus (http://www.tkga.com/preciouspals.shtm , www.projectlinus.org).

✦ Get the boys involved in collecting food that can be distributed locally through a food bank such as Second Harvest (www.secondharvest.org). Your local post office sponsors a "Stamp Out Hunger" food drive every May that you could also volunteer for (www.usps.com).

✦ Collect toys for needy children before the holidays so that they can be distributed through the Toys For Tots organization (www.toysfortots.org). Local soup kitchens often need toys for Christmas and Easter too.

✦ Talk to your stake presidency and see if they would be interested in inviting all of the Primary children in your ward or stake to participate in National Youth Service Day or USA Weekend's Make a Difference Day.

PRIMARILY FOR CUB SCOUTS

✦ Wash windows on the cars parked at the temple and leave little notes that thank the patrons for their service. Be careful of car alarms, and make sure you get permission from the temple presidency first!

✦ Make visual aids to give to the Primary teachers and chorister, such as flannel board stories, music aids, object lessons, and so forth. Laminate the pictures so they will last a long time. (Wolf Elective 12a, b, e)

✦ Have the boys help a new Scout memorize all of the items in the Bobcat Trail. (Webelos Scholar 13)

✦ Have the boys make thank you cards for the Cub Master and other leaders on the Scout Committee

✦ Hold an "Unsung Hero" service project. Find out who in the ward has "quiet" callings such as the librarian, Church magazine rep, choristers, pianists, bulletin board person, sacrament program printer, sacrament door greeters, and so forth. Invite them to a special dinner where you honor their efforts, and let them know they are appreciated.

✦ Put American flags on military tombstones on Memorial Day, Independence Day, or Veteran's Day. You can look up military cemeteries at www.cem.va.gov/. (Wolf Achievement 2a, c, d, e, f, g)

✦ Organize a Blood Drive by calling 1-800-GIVE-LIFE. The boys will not be allowed to actually donate their blood until age eighteen, but they can help out at the "canteen" by passing out refreshments to donors.

✦ Show support by attending community events. Help your boys get involved by making a float for a local parade, running in a 5K, passing out snacks at a craft fair, and so on.

✦ Adopt a specific military Troop to pray for by signing up at www.presidentialprayerteam.net/manageadoptionslogin.php. You can also sign up to send packages and letters to servicemen and women at www.anysoldier.com.

SERVING OTHERS

✦ Sign up to be clowns in a local parade and pass out candy to the children.

✦ Pack up all of your rubber stamping supplies, and visit the children's trauma unit in your local hospital. Help the patients decorate cards to give to their families, friends, the hospital staff, or to whomever they want to thank.

✦ Take old cards you have received or made, and cut the fronts off and send them to Gwen Mangelson. She and her volunteer team will turn them into new cards and donate them to the Ronald McDonald house. The patients use them to thank volunteers and to cheer up their sick friends.

> Gwen Mangelson
> RMH SU lead
> 323 Autumn Circle
> Rogersville, MO 65742

✦ Teach the boys how to make cinnamon rolls from scratch using different kinds of wheat (hard red, soft winter, and so forth.) Have them take home a batch for their families or make some for an early morning Seminary class.

✦ Create "Secret Grandmas." Get a list of all the older sisters in the ward and assign a few of the boys to each senior sister. Deliver secret gifts to them for a month. Bring them flowers, cards, goodies, and crafts. At the end of the month invite the senior sisters to a special presentation and reveal who their secret "grandsons" were. Share with them the definition of true religion found in James 1:27. (Wolf Elective 9b, c)

✦ The annual "Scouting for Food" service project is held nationwide in October, but you can hold a canned food drive any time of year. Divide the boys into teams and call ward members to let them know that during the next week, the boys will be stopping by to pick up donated canned food items. Have a contest to see who can collect the most.

✦ Many retirement homes have big bingo events that the boys could help with. You could also sing for the residents, make and bring gifts for them, help

PRIMARILY FOR CUB SCOUTS

them write letters to their families, and with permission, have the boys bring their pets for the residents to hold and play with. (Webelos Showman 1, 9, 11)

✦ Stuff envelopes for a school, PTA, charity, or some other non-profit organization. Talk about the importance of getting involved in school activities and what kinds of things you can learn by being an active participant in the community. (Webelos Scholar 3, 4, 5)

✦ Organize a special Military Appreciation Day or Welcome Home picnic for families in the service in your area. (Webelos Citizen 13, 15, 16, 17)

✦ Project Evergreen is a program which organizes volunteers to help a military family with yard work when they're loved one is away on a tour of duty. Check out the website: www.projectevergreen.com/gcft/. (Webelos Handyman 12, 14, 15)

✦ Make a list of chores the boys could do around their house and encourage them to do one during the next week to serve their families. (Wolf Achievement 4e; Webelos Family Member 1, 2, 9, 10, 11; Webelos Handyman 1a, b, c)

✦ Invite the missionaries to speak about their choice to serve a full-time mission. Discuss how they prepared and the blessings that followed. Have everyone bring non-perishable items to include in care packages for missionaries, as well as for military servicemen and women who are serving from your ward. Include uplifting letters. (Webelos Citizen 16, 17)

✦ Make "Welcome to the Area" packets for new move-ins in your ward or branch. Include maps of the area, phone numbers, a ward directory, school and utility information, Parks & Recreation catalogs, and transportation routes and timetables. (Webelos Traveler 1, 2, 3, 9, 10, Academics Belt Loop for Map, Compass, Academic Belt Loop for Geography)

✦ Make gifts the boys could give to military servicemen and women on Veteran's Day or Memorial Day such as a patriotic craft, plaque, cookies, an award, and thank-you cards. Invite a Veteran to speak to the boys about his or

SERVING OTHERS

her experience serving this country. (Webelos Citizen 11, 13, 14, 15, 16)

✦ Arrange to have your boys give three-minute talks in sharing time about the importance of service. (Webelos Communicator 2; Webelos Showman 1, 16)

✦ Using clean, dry soup cans or those big #10 food storage cans, paint designs on the outside and fill with treats that can be given to others as gifts. (Wolf Elective 9b, c; Webelos Artist 3)

✦ Teach the boys how to give themselves MANicures (how to correctly cut their fingernails). Talk about all of the good service we can do with our hands and how we can place our lives in God's hands. Go to www.actsweb.org, and read the story about the statue of Christ in Strasbourg and what happened to its hands during WWII. Using the boys' handprints, paint T-shirts, pots, binders, make plaster of paris designs, or other items. (Wolf 3a, b, c; Wolf Elective 3e, Webelos Badge Requirement 8a, b, c, d, e; Webelos Artist 3)

✦ Arrange to visit an animal shelter to play with the animals and help clean up the stalls. Talk about the importance of respecting wildlife. (Wolf Elective 14a, b, c, d; Webelos Handyman 1a, b, 11, 14, 15, 16, 17; Webelos Naturalist 1a, b, c, 12)

✦ Read children's stories into a tape recorder and package the books and tapes together as a set so they can be given to a hospital, Boys & Girls Club, library, preschool, school for the blind, or daycare center. (Wolf Elective 6a, b, c; Webelos Communicator 6; Webelos Scholar 3, 4, 5)

✦ Find out how your boys can participate in the March of Dimes Walk, the Children's Miracle Network programs, or some other local event to help fight terrible diseases. If Webelos walk three miles they also fulfill the requirement for Outdoorsman 9. (Webelos Athlete 5e)

✦ Talk to the Parks and Recreation Facilities and Public Works Department of your city to see what service projects your boys could do. They can usually

PRIMARILY FOR CUB SCOUTS

think of ideas that would readily qualify as service, such as painting over graffiti or cleaning up parks.

✦ Talk to your bishop to see if the Primary could get involved in the Adopt-a-Highway or Adopt-a-Waterway programs. These projects require a prolonged commitment, so you need to make sure there is serious follow-through and that the bishop is the contact person in case current Cub Scout and Primary leaders are released and given other callings. Learn about the aquatic ecosystem in your area. ("Leave No Trace" Awareness Award, World Conservation, Naturalist 1a, b, c, 9, 11)

✦ Paint and wallpaper a shelter. Hardware stores may be willing to donate supplies if you just ask. (Webelos Artist 3)

✦ Write to your local congressman about issues that affect your community. Invite a local civic leader to speak about how the scouts can contribute in a positive way. Write letters of appreciation to congressmen for setting such a great example of leadership. (Wolf Elective 21b; Bear Achievement 17 e; Webelos Citizen 1, 2, 10, 15, 16, 17; Communicator 8, 11, 12, 13)

✦ Teach the boys some sign language and check out the Church's web site about American Sign Language at www.asl.lds.org. See if there is a school for deaf children nearby where the boys could help out and practice their new skills. (Wolf Elective 1c; Webelos Communicator 3, 5; Webelos Scholar 3, 4, 5; Academics Belt Loop for Language and Culture)

✦ Find out if there are some projects with Habitat for Humanity that your boys could help with. Young children are not allowed to work on dangerous construction, but they could help prepare and serve refreshments or other tasks. For more information go to www.habitat.org.

✦ Surprise everyone in your church building by cleaning it! Tackle the kitchen and make labels for the cabinets, organizing their contents and cleaning the shelves. Reserve a cabinet or box for lost and found items. (Webelos Handyman 1a, b, 11, 14)

✦ Teach the boys how to make a quilt that could be given to a shelter, a high school senior leaving for college, a new baby in the ward, or someone in need.

✦ Go to the Family Home Storage Center and can food for families in the ward who are unable to do the manual labor themselves. Check with your local cannery to find out about age restrictions on operating equipment. Most likely, your boys will not be able to use the equipment, but they could get a tour of the facility and prepare boxes and label cans for patrons.

✦ Invite a representative from the Red Cross to teach the boys about disaster relief, preparedness, and how the Cub Scouts can help in your community. (Wolf Elective 16a, b, c; Webelos Readyman 15)

✦ Do something nice for the bishopric or presidencies of each auxiliary in your ward to let them know their hard work is appreciated. (Wolf 11c,d)

✦ Help your ward's activity director prepare for the next party or event by making decorations, centerpieces, posters, and so forth. (Wolf 11c, d; Wolf Elective 3a, e; Wolf Elective 9a; Academic Belt Loop for Art, Academic Belt Loop for Communicating)

✦ Create a "Taste the Sweetness of Service" jar by giving a specially decorated jar to the bishop. Primary children can visit his office and put a piece of candy in the jar when they give acts of service. (Wolf Elective 9b, c; 11c, d)

✦ Do yard work for a widow in your ward, the elderly, or someone on bed-rest. (Bear Elective 14a, c; Webelos Handyman 1, 13, 14)

✦ Sing the Seven Dwarves song "Hi Ho" but have it stand for something new—Happiness Is Helping Others. (Wolf Elective 11c, d; Webelos Showman 1, 9, 11; Academic Belt Loop for Music)

Primarily for Cub Scouts

+ Host a Wizard of Oz–themed event to talk about getting the heart, head, and courage to do service. (Wolf 11 c, d)

+ Invite ward members who are widows, elderly, or home-bound to join the "Letter a Month Club." Prepare cards and letters that could then be mailed every month to uplift and inspire them. (Wolf 11c, d; Elective 21b; Webelos Communicator 11)

+ Put together "Finals Survival Kits" to send to college students from your ward. Include a bag of "brain candy" and encouraging letters to help them get through those long study hours. (Wolf 11c, d)

+ Plan a special dance for the married couples in the ward in the style of a prom, complete with photos, dinner, and crowning of a king and queen. (Wolf 11c, d)

+ Learn about literacy and the Church's emphasis on helping others to read. "Ye Shall Have My Words" is the name of the Church-produced literacy program. Offer to help students in a Boys & Girls Club, after-school facility, or members of your own ward. (Wolf Elective 6a, b; Webelos Scholar 1, 2, 3, 13)

+ Help the boys write thank-you notes on stationery they make. (Bear Achievement 18 e)

+ Plan a special luncheon for the Primary teachers and presidency to thank them for all they do for the children. (Wolf 11c, d)

+ Crochet leper bandages, baby caps, infant layettes, as well as other products used by the Church's Humanitarian Department. For more information contact:

    Latter-day Saint Humanitarian Center
    1665 Bennett Road
    SLC, UT 84104
    Telephone: (801) 240-6060
    Hours 8:00 AM - 4:00 PM, Monday through Friday

(Wolf 11c, d)

- Make newborn hats that can be donated to hospitals. Buy or make one of those round looms to make the project go very quickly and easily! You can also make larger hats for older cancer patients.

- Invite the boys to take their pets to a children's hospital or retirement home to visit with the residents. Be sure to check for allergies first! (Webelos Badge 8, Webelos Citizen 8)

- If you have artistic boys, take them to a retirement home or children's hospital and have them draw portraits of the residents. If they aren't very good at drawing you could take photographs that could be printed out and brought back on another day. (Wolf Elective 3a; Academic Belt Loop for Art)

- Take cookies to widows on Valentine's Day or other holidays. (Bear Achievement 9a)

- Create a service coupon book together that the boys can give as gifts to their families and friends. (Wolf 10a)

- Have a "Random Acts of Kindness" contest and see which team can do the most service in an hour. You could set it up like a scavenger hunt.

- Plan a dinner for all of the Seminary teachers and their spouses. (Wolf Achievement 8a, c, e; Wolf 11c, d)

- Decorate lunch bags for missionaries and fill them with yummy food and snacks to enjoy at zone conference. (Wolf 11c, d)

- Help an older person write an autobiography or organize photos. Record a video of him or her being interviewed. (Webelos Family Member 1)

- Make hospital gift tray items such as nice poems rolled up with a ribbon and piece of candy. (Wolf Achievement 9b, c)

- Make gift baskets to give to military wives on Mother's Day, Easter, or Christmas.

PRIMARILY FOR CUB SCOUTS

- Find out how your Cub Scouts and ward can help with Special Olympics events in your area.

- Build a Pinewood Derby track for your pack if your ward or stake doesn't have one. Instructions can be found at www.abc-pinewood-derby.com. (Webelos Craftsman 1, 2, 4; Webelos Handyman 12, 14, 15, 16, 17)

- Build toy boxes or shelves for your building's nursery or Primary room. (Wolf Achievement 5a, b, c, d, e; Wolf Elective 3a, e; Webelos Craftsman pin 1, 2, 4; Webelos Handyman 12, 13, 14, 15, 16, 17)

- Find out if there is an "Operation Sack Lunch" program in your area where the boys could help prepare and pass out lunches to the homeless in a safe facility.

- Using skills learned with tools, repair someone's fence or build something useful. (Wolf Achievement 5a, b, c, d, e; Wolf Elective 3a, e; Webelos Craftsman 1, 2, 3, 4; Webelos Handyman 12, 14, 15, 16, 17)

- Pick up litter in a neighborhood, at the park, or on a beach. (Wolf Achievement 7d; Bear Achievement 6g; World Conservation, "Leave No Trace" Awareness Award; Webelos Naturalist 12)

- Plan and cook a nutritious meal for a family in the ward who needs extra help, such as when there is a sickness in the family or a new baby. If the meal is cooked outdoors, then Webelos fulfill Outdoorsman 8. (Wolf Achievement 8a, b, c, d, e)

- Call the Relief Society president or compassionate service leader in your ward to find out if the boys could do yard work for someone who needs help. (Wolf 11c, d; Wolf Elective 8b; Bear Achievement 6g; Webelos Handyman 1, 13, 14, 15)

- Show Scout Spirit by participating in den or pack service projects. (Bobcat Trail; Wolf Achievement 6a; Wolf Achievement 10d; Wolf Elective 11c, f; Wolf

Elective 12f; Wolf Elective 23a, d, e, f, g, h; Bear Achievement 8b, c; Webelos Citizen 17)

IDEAS FROM THE FAITH IN GOD BOOKLET:

✦ Read and discuss the parable of the good Samaritan (see Luke 10:30–37). Plan and complete a service project that helps a family member or neighbor. After completing the project, discuss how it helped your faith grow stronger. (Wolf 7d; Bear 6g; Webelos Badge 8e; Webelos Family Member 5; Webelos Scholar 3, 13)

✦ Write a letter to a teacher, your parents, or your grandparents, telling them what you appreciate and respect about them. (If you use a computer— Wolf Elective 21b; Bear 18b, e and 24d; Webelos Communicator 11; Religious Knot patch)

✦ Make a list of the qualities you like in a person. Choose one quality to develop in yourself. Discuss how showing respect and kindness strengthens you, your family, and others. (Wolf 6a, 7a and e, 9a, 10a; Bear 8g, 24f; Webelos Naturalist 1; Webelos Scholar 1)

✦ Plan, prepare, and serve a nutritious meal. (Wolf 8; Bear 9c, g; Webelos Family Member 11; Webelos Fitness 3)

✦ Entertain young children with songs or games you have learned or made yourself. Show that you know how to care for and protect a young child. (Wolf 10b, Elective 4, Bear 10b, Webelos Family Member 8)

✦ Learn about and practice good manners and courtesy. (Wolf 4c, 10a; Bear 24d)

✦ Plan and hold a parent-child activity, such as a dinner, picnic, hike, day trip, or service project. (Wolf Elective 18a, b, c, d, e, 19c; Bear 10, 12, 14g, 15a, Elective 16d; Webelos Family Member 8; Webelos Outdoorsman 2)

PRIMARILY FOR CUB SCOUTS

✦ Read the twelfth article of faith. Discuss what it means to be a good citizen and how your actions can affect others. (Wolf Elective 11a, b; Bear 3j; Webelos Citizen 1, 4, 7, 8, 9, 12, 13, 14, 15)

✦ Help your Primary leaders plan and carry out an upcoming quarterly activity. (Wolf 11d, Elective 9a; Bear 24c; Religious Knot patch)

7

Developing Talents

Find out what the boys are interested in and plan activities that allow them to teach one another and shine. Whenever the boys learn about any of the suggestions listed below in a book, they'll be completing the requirement for Wolf Elective 6b.

✦ Create a "House Olympics." Have fun and silly competitions that test such skills as sewing a button, reading a story, making a sandwich, ironing a shirt, making a bed, and sweeping the floor. Include an Opening Ceremony with flags the boys design, have entertainment, and play the Olympic theme song. Talk about how learning these skills will better prepare them for missions and college. Talk about the importance of contributing to the family by helping with chores. (Wolf Achievement 4e; Webelos Family Member 1, 2, 9, 10; Webelos Handyman 1a, b, and c, 11; Academic Belt Loop for Citizens)

✦ Teach the boys what a melodrama is and then have them create one! Perform live or record their show on video. The cornier the better! Use this year's Primary theme, the Cub Scout theme, a scripture, Primary song, or make up lines or props they have to include in their play. (Wolf Achievement 2a; Webelos Showman 1, 19, 20)

✦ Teach the boys how to make different kinds of pizza: deep dish, vegetarian, fruit, dessert, thin crust, meat lovers, and so forth. Learn how to make different kinds of crust too: Boboli, hand-made, Bisquick, deep-dish, thin, or cookie.

PRIMARILY FOR CUB SCOUTS

- Have a "Handyman" class where you teach the boys how to fix a squeaky door and repair other household items. (Webelos Handyman 10, 11, 12, 16, 17)

- Start a book club or help the boys start one in their community, by choosing good books and creating a list of discussion items that could be included in a group setting. Have each boy present an oral book report on a book they liked. (Wolf Elective 6a, b; Webelos Showman 1, 16)

- Take the boys to their local library and help them get a card if they don't have one already. You may need to invite parents to join you to do this. Talk about the importance of reading good books throughout our lives. Collect books that could be donated to the library. (Wolf Elective 6a, b, c; Webelos Communicator 3, 5, 6, 12; Academic Belt Loop for Language and Culture)

- Teach the boys how to sew a patch on their uniform and talk about the importance of caring for their appearance. (Webelos Fitness 1)

- Role-play with phones to teach the boys proper telephone manners. (Wolf Achievement 4c)

- Teach the boys how to plan and cook a nutritious meal. If the meal is cooked outdoors then Webelos fulfill Outdoorsman 8. (Wolf Achievement 8a, b, c, d, e; Bear Achievement 9a, b, c, d ,e ,f g; Webelos Family 11; Webelos Fitness 3, 4)

- Encourage the boys' families to take a tour around their houses and create a safe home. The boys could prepare material to present a lesson about home safety for their next family home evening. (Wolf Achievement 4a, b, c, d; Wolf Achievement 9b, c, d; Wolf Elective 14 b, d; Wolf Elective 23c, d; Bear Achievement 7b, c, e, f; Bear Achievement 11a; Webelos Family Member 1, 6, 7, 9; Webelos Fitness 2; Webelos Readyman 3, 11, 13)

- Invite a nurse or doctor to teach the boys first aid skills. (Wolf Achievement 3c; Wolf Elective 16c; Webelos Readyman 2, 4, 5, 6, 7, 12, 15; Webelos Traveler 8, 11)

DEVELOPING TALENTS

◆ Learn about a historic place in your community and visit it as a den. (Wolf Achievement 4f; Bear Achievement 3c, d, e; Bear Achievement 4a, b; Bear Achievement 8e)

◆ Invite a dad to teach the boys all about tools, how to use them safely, and store them properly. A perfect time to do this is right before Pinewood Derby time when they will be using tools to build their cars. (Wolf Achievement 5a, b, c, d, e; Wolf Elective 3c; Bear Achievement 19a, b, c, d; Bear Achievement 20a, b, c; Bear Elective 4 a, c, d, e; Webelos Craftsman 1, 2, 3, 4; Webelos Handyman 14, 15, 16, 17)

◆ Invite the boys to bring items they have collected and help them organize their collection by creating labels. The boys could make a special box out of cardboard with small sections. Display the collections on a table at your next pack meeting. Show them how to care for a CD collection. (Wolf Achievement 6b, c; Bear Elective 12a, b, c, d, e, f, g; Webelos Showman 10; Academic Belt Loop for Collecting)

◆ Teach the boys about ecology and conservation. Teach them the Scout "Outdoor Code" and "Leave No Trace" pledge. Help the boys draw a poster to illustrate their pledge and display it at your next pack meeting. (Wolf Achievement 7b, c, d, e, f; Bear Achievement 6a, b, c, d, e, f, g; Bear Elective 12a, b, c, d, e, f, g, h; Webelos Badge Requirement 7; Leave No Trace Awareness Award 3; Arrow of Light 3; World Conservation Award, Academic Belt Loop for Communicating)

◆ Have the boys learn about bike safety before going on a bike ride. Teach them some simple bike repair skills. Help them create a safety notebook in order to fulfill Webelos Fitness pin 2. (Wolf Achievement 9e; Bear Achievement 14a, b, c, d, e, f, g; Webelos Athlete 8; Webelos Handyman 6, 7, 8; Webelos Readyman 9)

◆ Teach the boys how to do magic tricks that they could perform at a pack meeting for their families. Show them how to do fun balancing tricks and create optical illusions. (Wolf Elective 1b; Bear Elective 13a, b, c, d; Webelos Scientist 11, 12)

✦ Teach the boys about photography. If you live near a temple, they could learn how to take beautiful pictures of the temple grounds. (Bear Elective 11a, b, c, d)

✦ Learn about the American Indians together. Most cities have Native American clubs or performing groups you could invite to join you at your next pack meeting. (Wolf Elective 1d; Wolf Elective 2b; Wolf Elective 10a, b, c, d, e, f)

✦ Surely you have some thespians in your den. Well, at least some hams! Create a play or skit where the boys could show off their great acting talents at a pack meeting. Discuss Shakespeare, opera, musicals, and stage directions. Draw a picture of the famous Globe theater. Webelos need to read a play and make a model stage for some of the Showman requirements as well. Attend a play together. (Wolf Elective 2a, b, c, d; Webelos Showman 1, 17, 19, 20, 22, 23)

✦ Invite the boys to bring one of their pets from home for "Show and Tell." Hold a pet parade outside. Talk about the importance of pet care. Be sure to have a pooper scooper on hand! (Wolf Elective 14 a, b, Bear Achievement 5 a, b, Webelos Showman 1, 16)

✦ Take a nature hike and learn about nature and plants. Make a bingo board for each boy that shows pictures of possible plants you may see on your hike and have the boys cross them off as they see them. Webelos who draw or paint an outdoor picture fulfill Artist Badge 3. If the hike lasts for three miles, then Webelos also fulfill Outdoorsman 9. (Wolf Elective 18e, g; Bear Achievement 5c; Bear Elective 12a, b, c, d, e, f, g, h; Webelos Badge Requirement, Webelos Naturalist 1a, b, c, 6, 7, 8, 9, 10; Arrow of Light 5; Academic Belt Loop for Art; Academic Belt Loop for Wildlife Conservation)

✦ Have each of the boys give a three-minute talk at a den meeting about some talents they have developed. (Webelos Communicator 2; Webelos Showman 1, 16)

✦ Invite the dads to join you and teach the boys about fishing as you take a field trip to a local lake, river, or hatchery. (Wolf Elective 19a, b, c, d, e, f; Bear Achievement 5c; Webelos Traveler 1, 2, 3, 4, 5, 6, 7, 9, 10)

✦ The boys are probably already comfortable playing on a computer, but invite your local "computer expert" to teach them something they don't know. Visit one of the the Church's web sites such as www.lds.org or www.providentliving.org. If you have a missionary serving from your ward, you could visit the website www.dearelder.com and write him or her a letter. Make an art project using the computer and talk about careers in computer science or communication. (Wolf Elective 21a, b, c; Bear Achievement 17d, e; Webelos Artist 5; Webelos Communicator 11, 12, 13, 16; Academic Belt Loop for Communicating; Academic Belt Loop for Computers)

✦ Teach the boys about model rockets, build them, and shoot them off! (Webelos Scientist 5, 6, 7, 8)

✦ The boys are probably learning about your state at school, so invite them to share what they know. Ask each boy to draw a picture of the state flag, state flower, or state bird. Write a letter to your state governor about an issue they think is important. (Wolf Achievement 4f; Wolf Elective 6b; Wolf Elective 22d; Bear Achievement 3a, c, d; Bear Achievement 4a; Bear Achievement 6c; Bear Achievement 8e; Webelos Citizen 1, 7, 10, 13; Webelos Communicator 8, 11, 12, 13; Webelos Naturalist 5, 6; Webelos Scholar 2, 4, 5; Academic Belt Loop for Communicating)

✦ Talk about how the boys can be good citizens in their city, state, and country. Discuss their rights and responsibilities. Share stories about people who are good citizens. (Webelos Badge Requirement 5; Webelos Citizen 1a, b, c; 12, 13, 15; Arrow of Light 3)

PRIMARILY FOR CUB SCOUTS

✦ Find a local lake where the boys can learn how to sail. (Bear Elective 5a, b, c, d, e)

✦ Visit a local airport and see if they offer free tours to teach the boys about aircraft. (Bear Elective 6a, b, c, d, e, f, g)

✦ Invite an artist or art teacher to teach the den about different occupations in the art field. (Webelos Artist 1)

✦ Invite a Boy Scout to teach the boys the proper way to use a knife. The older boy will be able to pass off requirements for his "Tote N Chip" award and your Cub Scout will pass off Bear Achievement 19a, b, c, d.

✦ Introduce the boys to model building. Webelos who build a model of a stage fulfill Showman 1, 18. (Bear Achievement 21a, b, c, d, e, f; Bear Elective 1d; Bear Elective 6d, g)

✦ Find out which of the boys know how to play a musical instrument and organize a talent show where they can perform for their families at a pack meeting, for the den, or during sharing time in Primary. Teach the boys how to play a simple song on an instrument if they haven't had any musical training. If they do play an instrument, encourage them to learn how to play a hymn or Primary song. (Wolf Elective 10b, d; Wolf Elective 11a, b, c, d, e, f; Bear Elective 8a, b, c, d; Webelos Showman 1, 8, 11, 13, 14; Academic Belt Loop for Music)

✦ Offer a leadership position to each boy and help them develop skills such as conducting a den meeting, planning an activity, or leading the music. (Bear Achievement 24e; Webelos Scholar 1, 2, 3)

✦ Invite speakers from the local hospital to teach babysitter certification classes to your boys. (Webelos Family Member 6, 9; Webelos Fitness 2; Webelos Readyman 11, 13, 15)

✦ Teach your boys all about weather and do fun experiments about atmospheric air and water pressure. Create fog in a bottle and crystals using instructions found online at www.weatherwizkids.com. (Webelos Scientist 5, 6, 7, 9, 10, 13; Academic Belt Loop for Weather)

✦ Show the boys how to search online for more information about an area they're interested in. (Webelos Communicator 12; Academic Belt Loop for Computers)

✦ Create a "Mad Scientist" activity where the boys can do science experiments. Check out all of the ideas listed at www.funology.com. (Webelos Scientist; Academic Belt Loop for Science.)

✦ Teach the boys how to do basic car maintenance such as changing a tire, replacing a tail light, checking oil level and tire pressure, and washing a car. (Webelos Handyman 2, 3, 4, 5)

✦ Help the boys develop their creative talents by encouraging them to participate in their school's annual "Reflections" contest held nationwide. For more information check out www.pta.org. (Webelos Artist 3, 4, 5, 6, 7, 8, 9, 10; Academics Belt Loop for Art)

✦ Learn how to make piñatas or other papier-mâché items. Talk about what we can learn from other cultures and their traditions. Learn which ethnic groups exist in your community. (Bear Achievement 3c, d; Bear Achievement 4a, b)

✦ Visit the city hall or the community recreation center and have the boys learn about their town. (Bear Achievement 3c, d; Bear Achievement 4a, b; Webelos Citizen 1, 2, 7, 10, 11, 12, 13, 15, 16, 17)

✦ On several national holidays, you could teach the boys about great leaders in history as you do a patriotic craft. (Bear Achievement 3b; Webelos Artist 9; Citizen 1, 11, 12, 13, 14, 15, 16, 17)

✦ Teach the boys how to cook something and then give them a recipe they can add to their growing collection. Have the boys decorate a recipe book or folder. Create dividers based on categories the boys want to learn about, such as breads, things to do with pumpkins (after the fall holidays), desserts, chicken dishes, appetizers, fun drinks, or campout meals. (Wolf Elective 8c, d, e; Webelos Family Member 11; Webelos Fitness 3, 4; Webelos Outdoorsman 8; Academic Belt Loop for Collecting)

✦ Invite your Ward Emergency Preparedness Specialist to teach a lesson on how to be better prepared for emergencies. Have the boys put together an emergency car kit, first aid kit, or something they could add to their family's 72-hour home kit. Show what kinds of tools could be stored in a car for emergencies too. (Wolf Achievement 41; Wolf Elective 16a, b, c; Bear Achievement 7d, e; Bear Achievement 11a, b, c, d, e; Webelos Handyman 5, 15, 16, 17; Webelos Readyman 2, 4, 5, 6, 7, 12, 15; Webelos Traveler 8, 11)

✦ Teach the boys about balance and how to walk on stilts or tin can shoes. (Wolf Elective 7a, b, c)

✦ Take the boys on a field trip to learn about different kinds of machines. (Wolf Elective 8a, b, c, d; Webelos Traveler 1, 2, 3, 4, 5, 6, 7, 9, 10)

✦ Teach the boys how to make a sculpture out of clay. (Webelos Artist 7)

✦ Invite speakers from your local "Toast Masters Club" or high school Speech & Debate team to teach the boys how to prepare an effective Primary talk. Practice giving a talk and then coordinate with your Primary presidency to assign talks the boys could give during sharing time. Practice giving a talk. (Webelos Showman 1, 16)

✦ Learn how to do outdoor cooking such as Dutch oven cooking or barbecue. Have a contest with the Boy Scouts to see who can cook the best main course or dessert. (Wolf Achievement 8e; Webelos Family Member 11; Webelos Fitness 3, 4; Webelos Outdoorsman 8)

✦ Take a field trip to the zoo and learn about animals. Discuss the importance of respecting wildlife and the balance of nature. (Bear Achievement 5a, c, d, e; Webelos Naturalist 1a, b, c, 4, 6, 7, 8, 9, 10, 11; Webelos Traveler 1, 2, 3, 4,

DEVELOPING TALENTS

5, 6, 7, 9, 10; Academics Belt Loop Map & Compass; Academic Belt Loop for Wildlife Conservation)

✦ Organize a career fair or have the boys attend one where they can hear people talk about different kinds of jobs. It would also be fun to invite the boys' parents to a den meeting where they could share what they do for a living. (Bear Achievement 17f; Webelos Family Member 1)

✦ Visit the police station in your area. Most stations offer a short tour of their facilities and usually the officers are more than happy to talk to the boys. (Wolf Elective 22d; Bear Achievement 7a, b, c, d ,e, f; Webelos Citizen 9)

✦ Invite the boys to come prepared to share a story. Some libraries offer storytelling time. Teach them how to become effective storytellers. (Bear Achievement 4a, b, c; Webelos Showman 1, 16; Academic Belt Loop for Communicating)

✦ Learn about birds. Try to duplicate bird sounds and go bird watching. (Wolf Elective 13a, b, c, d, e, f; Bear Achievement 5a, b, c, d; Bear Elective 12h; Webelos Naturalist 1a, b, c, 5, 6, 9, 10)

✦ Learn how to plant and care for a garden, as well as take care of yard tools. Take a field trip to a community garden or visit someone who has a great garden. Talk about the wisdom in the prophet's counsel to plant a garden. (Wolf Elective 15a, b, c, d; Bear Achievement 6b; Bear Elective 14a, b, c, d; Webelos Handyman 1a, b, c, 13, 14, 15, 16, 17; Webelos Traveler 1, 2, 3, 4, 5, 6, 9, 10)

✦ Take the boys to your local Family History Center to learn about genealogy. (Bear Achievement 8d; Webelos Family Member 1; Academic Belt Loop for Heritages)

✦ Invite an older Boy Scout to teach the boys how to tie knots. He'll be able to pass off some of his requirements and so will your boys. (Wolf Elective 17a, b, d, e, f, g; Bear Achievement 22a, b, c, d, e, f; Bear Elective 13d; Webelos Badge Requirement 2; Arrow of Light 2)

PRIMARILY FOR CUB SCOUTS

- Take a field trip to a recycling center to learn how one works and how it benefits the environment. A great fundraiser for the Scouting program is to encourage the boys to bring their recyclables to each den and pack meeting. It's amazing how much the paid redemption on those items adds up. (Wolf Achievement 7c, d, e, f; Bear Achievement 6a, c, d, e, f, g; World Conservation Award; Webelos Traveler 1, 2, 3, 4, 5, 6, 9, 10)

- Invite your Stake webmaster to talk about the resources available on the Church's website and how to use them. Find out if your ward has its own website and see what's on it. Create a website together for your pack. (Wolf Elective 21a, b, c; Webelos Communicator 12, Academic Belt Loop for Computers)

- Teach the boys how to sew. Have them make beanbags for games played in den meetings or for their own family home evenings.

- Learn how to bake bread. Reserve two or three loaves for next Sunday's sacrament meeting. (Webelos Badge Requirement 8e; Webelos Citizen 8)

- Learn about reflexology and how to care for feet and toenails. Talk about standing in holy places, "how beautiful are the feet of those who spread the gospel," and discuss what we can learn when the Savior washed the disciples' feet. (Webelos Athlete 2, 3; Webelos Fitness 1a, b, c)

- Teach about trees by taking a field trip to a forest. Identify forest plants, trees, soil, wood, and tree rings. Talk about wildfire prevention in your area and draw some of the pictures required to earn the Webelos Forester pin. (Webelos Traveler 1, 2, 3, 4, 5, 6, 7, 9, 10, 11)

- Teach the boys to be "street smart" to protect themselves. Introduce them to some of the following web sites:

www.vcpionline.org/mousetrap.asp
www.netsmartz.org
www.missingkids.com
www.familywatchdog.us/

[Bobcat 8; Wolf Achievement 9b, c, d, e; Webelos Fitness 2]

✦ If your Primary doesn't have those cute fabric seat covers that identify each Primary class on the back of their chairs, teach your boys how to sew them. Present them to your Primary during sharing time. [Wolf Achievement 11 d]

✦ Teach the boys how to play volleyball. Discuss sports signals, counting points, and sportsmanship. [Sports Volleyball Belt Loop; Webelos Sportsman 1 2, 3, 4]

✦ Learn about other countries. Invite returned missionaries to give mini-lessons on the country where they served. Create a travel box where the boys can store special vacation photos and souvenirs by decoupaging maps, postcards, and other travel memorabilia. Help the boys learn to read a map. [Wolf Achievement 5e; Webelos Traveler 1, 9, 10; Academic Belt Loop Map & Compass; Academic Belt Loop for Geography; Academic Belt Loop for Language and Culture]

✦ Learn all about sports and have an outdoor game day. Earn one of the Sports belt loops together. [Bear Achievement 15a; Bear Achievement 23a, b, c, e; Webelos Sportsman 1, 2, 3, 4]

✦ Teach the boys about geology by examining fossils and rocks. Make a drawing of a volcano and then build one that uses baking soda, vinegar, and red food coloring to create bubbly lava. [Webelos Geologist 1-9; Academic Belt Loop for Geology]

✦ Take a field trip to your local planetarium, science museum, or college where they might have telescopes and exhibits on outer space. The boys could make a mobile of the solar system made out of painted Styrofoam balls. [Bear Elective 1a, b, c, d, e, f; Webelos Artist 3, 8; Webelos Traveler 1, 2, 3, 4, 5, 6, 9, 10; Academic Belt Loop for Astronomy; Academic Belt Loop for Science]

✦ Find out which boys are good at skateboarding and have them teach the

PRIMARILY FOR CUB SCOUTS

others how to do it. Learn how to change the wheels on a skateboard or inline skates. (Webelos Handyman 9)

✦ Find an expert who could teach the boys about airwaves and how radios work. Find out if your ward or stake has a ham radio operator who could show the boys some equipment and talk about how helpful it can be during emergencies. Your local TV and radio station might even have a free tour for the public. Discuss careers in the field of communications. (Bear Elective 3a, b; Webelos Communicator 6, 7; Webelos Citizen 9, 17; Webelos Readyman 3; Academic Belt Loop for Communicating)

✦ Take a ride together using public transportation. Some boys may never have been inside a train or bus! Invite each boy to make a poster that teaches about a different form of transportation. (Bear Elective 7a, b, c, d; Webelos Traveler 1, 2, 3, 4, 5, 6, 7, 8, 9, 10, 11; Academic Belt Loop for Communicating)

✦ Invite an electrician to talk to the boys about what he does and discuss careers in his field. Help the boys construct a simple electrical circuit using a battery and wires. Show them how to make a potato clock they can take home. It's always a big hit! Learn how at www.ehow.com (Webelos Engineer 5, 6)

✦ Invite the mayor or a city council member to teach the boys how your local government works. Attend a city council meeting or visit your city hall and meet the people who work there. They often will allow your den to conduct the flag ceremony before a town hall meeting. (Wolf Achievement 2a, b, c, d, e, f, g; Wolf Achievement 4f; Bear Achievement 3g, f, h, I; Webelos Badge Requirement 6; Webelos Citizen 1a, b, c, 2, 3, 4, 5, 10, 13, 14, 15, 16, 17)

✦ Take a field trip to a construction site and invite a builder or surveyor to show the boys what he does. Learn about property lines and architecture. Help the boys draw a floor plan of their houses. (Webelos Engineer 2, 3, 4; Webelos Traveler 1, 2, 3, 4, 5, 6, 9, 10)

✦ Invite boys who are in middle school to sit as a panel of speakers to answer questions about their school, emphasizing the importance of education and choosing good friends. (Wolf Achievement 12a, b, c, d, e, f, g, h, i, j, k; Webelos Scholar 1a, b, c, 2, 3, 4, 5)

✦ Invite someone from a local bicycle store to teach the boys how to choose the right bike and how to take care of it. Learn how to do simple repairs such as lubricating the chain and inflating the tires. Go on a bike ride together. Find out if an amateur racing team in your town would be willing to give a presentation on what they do. (Wolf Achievement 9a, d, e; Webelos Athlete 8; Webelos Handyman 6, 7, 8, 15, 16, 17)

✦ Teach the boys some sign language and check out the Church's website about American Sign Language at www.asl.lds.org. Invite someone who is deaf to talk to the boys. (Wolf Elective 1c, d; Webelos Communicator 1, 3, 4, 5, 9; Academic Belt Loop for Language and Culture)

✦ Play "Scripture Clues at the Mall." Help the boys think harder about the scriptures in a fun way. Divide them into small teams and provide each group a set of scriptures and scripture reference clues that will direct them to various stores in the mall where they get a leader's signature before going to the next location. Meet at the food court for refreshments. (Webelos Athlete 1; Webelos Communicator 5)

✦ Help the boys set up an aquarium or terrarium to keep in their home for a month, using clear soda bottles. You can find instructions at www.stormthecastle.com. (Webelos Naturalist 1a, b, c, 3)

✦ Teach the boys different styles of dance: western line-dance, hip hop, Hawaiian stick dance, and so on. Think *America's Best Dance Crew*. Choreograph a fun routine that could be performed at a quarterly Primary Activity or in a ward road show. (Wolf Elective 23 g; Webelos Showman 1, 11)

✦ Make a funny music video to a Primary song or a song by an LDS artist. (Wolf Elective 23 g; Webelos Showman 1, 11; Academic Belt Loop for Music)

Primarily for Cub Scouts

✦ Learn what it takes to put a play or concert together by attending a dress rehearsal of a local show. You'll be able to get in free or else at a greatly reduced price and probably be able to meet the performers afterward. (Wolf Achievement 10f; Webelos Showman 1, 17)

✦ Read or act out the parable of the talents in Matthew 25 and talk about how we can develop our own talents. Encourage the boys to identify their unique talents, as well as the ones they'd like to develop. (Wolf Achievement 2a, b, c, d, e)

✦ Learn about some of the unusual sports in the Olympics such as curling or rugby. Earn one of the Sports Belt Loops together. (Wolf Elective 20o; Webelos Sportsman 1, 2, 3, 4)

✦ Learn about healthy habits and why it is important to take care of your body. Invite a nurse or doctor to share health information and how it applies to the Word of Wisdom. Do some exercises together. (Wolf Achievement 3a; Webelos Badge Requirement 5; Webelos Athlete 1-7, Webelos Fitness 1, 5, 6, 7, 8; Arrow of Light 3)

✦ Spend time in a pool doing aquarobics, snorkeling, and playing pool-games. Place items at the bottom of the pool and have the boys retrieve them. Include lifesaving skills and water safety instruction. Webelos who make a safety notebook also fulfill requirement 2 for the Fitness pin. (Wolf Achievement 1h, i; Bear Achievement 11b; Webelos Aquanaut 1, 2, 3, 4, 5, 7; Webelos Athlete 9; Webelos Readyman 8; Swimming Belt Loop)

✦ Help the boys set up an insect zoo in a clear soda bottle with tiny air holes. Learn what insects eat and how they live. (Webelos Naturalist 1a, b, and c; 2)

✦ Help Webelos learn all about Boy Scouts and the difference between the Webelos uniform in Cub Scouts and the Boy Scout uniform they'll be wearing once they advance. (Webelos Badge Requirement 4, 7; Arrow of Light 2)

✦ Invite an engineer to talk to the boys about careers in his field. Using

Developing Talents

pretzels, marshmallows, and other food materials, have the boys build a crane, bridge, or catapult. (Webelos Engineer 1, 7, 8, 9)

Ideas from the Faith in God Booklet:

♦ Developing Talents: (Complete at least two of the following activities each year)

♦ Learn how to budget and save money. Discuss why it is important to faithfully pay our tithing and how Heavenly Father blesses us when we do (see 3 Nephi 24:10–11). (Bear 13c, g, E21; Webelos Family Member 3, 4, 7, 8)

♦ Pay your tithing and begin saving for a mission. (Bear 13b)

♦ Learn to sing, play, or lead a song from the Children's Songbook. Teach or share the song in a family home evening or at Primary. Discuss how developing talents helps prepare us for service to Heavenly Father and others. (Wolf Elective 11d, e, f; Bear 1b, Elective 8b, d; Webelos Showman 8, 9, 14)

♦ Write a poem, story, or short play that teaches a principle of the gospel or is about Heavenly Father's creations. (Wolf 11, E2, Elective 21b; Bear 18f; Webelos Showman 2, 19, Religious knot patch)

♦ Make an item from wood, metal, fabric, or other material, or draw, paint, or sculpt a piece of art. Display your finished work for others to see. (Wolf 5e, Elective 3a, Elective 5b, c, d, e, f, g, h, i, Elective 7b, c, Elective 8d, Elective 9b, c, Elective 10b, c, d, e; Elective 12a, b, d, e, f; Bear 5b, 19c, 20b, 21a, b, d, f, Elective 1b, d, Electve 2b, c, Elective 6d, g, Elective 8a, Elective 9a, c, Elective 10, Elective 12, Elective 18b; Webelos Artisit 3, 5, 6, 7, 8, 9, 10, 11; Webelos Craftsman; Webelos Engineer 7, 8, 9)

♦ Visit an art museum or attend a concert, play, or other cultural event. Share your experience with your family or Activity Day group. (Wolf 10f; Bear 10a, Elective 9b; Webelos Showman 17; Webelos Traveler 4)

PRIMARILY FOR CUB SCOUTS

✦ Read D&C 88:118. Discuss what it means to "seek learning, even by study and also by faith." Improve your personal study habits by doing such things as learning how to choose and read good books or being prepared for school each day. (Wolf Elective 6b; Webelos Scholar 2, 4, 5)

✦ List five things you can do to help around your home. Discuss the importance of obeying and honoring your parents and learning how to work. (Wolf 4a, d, e, 7f, 9b, c, Elective 14a, Elective 15a, b, c, d, Elective 16; Bear 7e, 11, 13a, 16a, 18a, Elective 17, Elective 21b; Webelos Family Member 2, 9, 10, 11, 13; Webelos Handyman; Webelos Readyman)

✦ Plan a physical fitness program for yourself that may include learning to play a sport or game. Participate in the program for one month. (Wolf 1a, h, j, Elective 20; Bear 14b, f, 15a, 16, 18c, 23a,b,c, Elective 20; Webelos Athlete; Webelos Sportsman 2,3,4)

✦ Learn about and practice good nutrition, good health, and good grooming, including modest dress. (Wolf 3a; Bear 9d; Webelos Athlete 2, 3; Webelos Fitness 1, 3, 4)

8
Preparing for the Priesthood

Most boys are thrilled to graduate from Primary yet are a bit apprehensive about joining the older teenage boys. There is a big difference between the needs, interests, and maturity levels of an eleven-year-old Cub Scout and an Eagle Scout of seventeen! Eleven-year-old Scouts are technically Boy Scouts, but not yet in the Young Men program. They can often feel a little misplaced since they still have one foot in Primary and one foot in young man status. Here are a few ideas that will help them be prepared as well as excited for this important transition in their lives:

✦ Talk to the boys about wearing and caring for their Boy Scout uniform. Ask them what they think the "uniform" of a priesthood holder is. Invite some deacons to share their transition experiences with the boys or answer questions in a panel format.

✦ Teach the boys some camp songs before summer camp so they'll feel comfortable joining in on the fun once they get there. (Webelos Outdoorsman 2; Webelos Showman 1, 9, 11; Academic Belt Loop for Music)

✦ Help the boys memorize the Young Men theme so they don't feel awkward on Sunday when all of the other Young Men are saying it aloud together during opening exercises (if your ward does that).

✦ Give each graduating boy a "Young Men Survival Kit" that includes the

Young Men theme on a bookmark for his scriptures, the Boy Scout manual and kerchief, and a welcome letter from the bishopric and scoutmaster.

✦ Work with the Young Men presidency to create a "Welcome" packet that includes all of the Young Men materials and welcome letters from the leaders and older boys.

✦ Work with the Young Men presidency to assign a "Big Brother" from one of the Young Men to make sure he has someone to sit next to during opening exercises, knows about the activities, gets some fun treats or surprises in his mailbox, teaches him about the programs, and introduces him to the other Young Men.

✦ Coordinate a visit between a Young Men leader and the parents of the soon-to-be Boy Scout to explain all the ins and outs of the Young Men program. For a first-time Young Men parent, it can be overwhelming!

✦ Invite the Young Men to a "get-to-know-you" activity so they can get to know the other boys better.

✦ Invite the Young Men presidency and Boy Scouts to speak about how their organization works. You could have a panel atmosphere so that the boys could ask them questions about the similarities and differences of the two organizations.

✦ Take the eleven-year-old boys on a "field trip" to attend Young Men's one Sunday. The next week talk about the similarities and differences between the two programs. Ask the boys what they could learn and contribute to the Young Men group. Point out what talents and gifts they could offer so they feel valued and needed.

✦ Encourage the boys who will be turning twelve to attend the annual "Priesthood Preview" event in your ward or stake. The ward or stake Primary presidency is in charge of planning it. It should include a presentation on the priesthood, introduction of leaders, and explanation of the Young Men program. If the group is small, parents can talk about their sons and express love. The boys should return home feeling loved and excited to receive the priesthood and a greater desire to become effective servants of the Lord. (Wolf Achievement 6a; Wolf Achievement 7a; Wolf Achievement 9a; Webelos Scholar 1a, b, c)

✦ Talk about the importance of character, respect, and a positive attitude while preparing to receive the priesthood. Invite some of the older boys in the Young Men program to share what helped them prepare and what their responsibilities are now. (Wolf Achievement 6a; Wolf Achievement 7a; Wolf Achievement 9a; Webelos Scholar 1a, b, c)

✦ Teach the boys how to tie a necktie to wear to Church on Sunday. Have a race to see who can put one on the fastest. Talk about the importance of proper attire when participating in priesthood ordinances like passing the Sacrament. (Wolf Elective 17f)

✦ Invite the boys to give a three-minute talk in sharing time or during a den meeting about how to prepare for the priesthood. (Webelos Communicator 2; Webelos Showman 1, 16)

✦ Give each of your Cub Scouts an assignment where they can show and develop leadership skills so they will be prepared to serve in quorum presidencies in the Young Men program. As often as possible, invite the boys to conduct your den meetings and lead games and activities. (Wolf Elective 24e)

IDEAS FROM THE FAITH IN GOD BOOKLET:

✦ Preparing For the Priesthood: (These activities are to be completed when the boy is eleven years old. LDS boys join the "11-year-old Boy Scout" program; therefore, no Cub Scout requirements are passed off when these are completed.)

✦ Learn about the restoration of the Aaronic Priesthood (see D&C 13, D&C 107:20, and Joseph Smith—History 1:68–73).

✦ Read D&C 20:57-60 and Aaronic Priesthood: Fulfilling Our Duty to God, page 7. Discuss with a parent or leader the purposes of the Aaronic Priesthood and what it means to do your duty to God.

✦ Read D&C 88:77-80, D&C 88:118 and D&C 130:19. Discuss with a parent or Primary leader how important a good education is and how it can help strengthen you as a priesthood holder in your home and family and in the Church.

✦ Read "The Family: A Proclamation to the World." Make a list of things you can do to help strengthen your family and make a happy home. Share the list with your parents or Primary leader.

Graduating Boys

As the boys graduate from Primary, there are some special things you can do for them to let them know you are proud of them and that they will be missed:

✦ Present the graduating boy with a faux pearl in a velvet drawstring bag and tell him that he is a "pearl of great price"!

✦ Present the graduating boy with an oil lamp or flashlight to let him know that you appreciate how he has been a shining example to all of the other boys.

✦ Have a "Graduating Guys" moment in sharing time or at a pack meeting where you spotlight each boy and his accomplishments.

✦ Invite the boys in your pack to write a letter of appreciation for the graduating boys and put them in a specially-decorated binder with photos of everyone. (Webelos Communicator 11, Academic Belt Loop for Communicating)

✦ Hang pictures of all the graduating boys on a Primary bulletin board with information about their accomplishments.

- Give the graduating boy a picture of your nearest temple and a bag with some things he'll need now that he gets to do baptisms at the temple, such as a comb, picture of Christ, journal, a book about the temple, and so forth.

- Make a "Spiritual Survival Kit" that includes a bookmark, a journal, a list of favorite scriptures that all of the other boys have written down, an uplifting book about prayer, a picture of the Savior, and so forth. (Webelos Badge Requirement 8e)

- Invite the Primary presidency, the graduating boys, and their parents to a special lunch or dinner.

- Present the graduating boy with a photo album of all the pictures you've taken of him during his Primary years. That's a hint for you to remember to take a lot of pictures!

- Visit a Boy Scout Troop meeting with all of your graduating boys. (Webelos Badge Requirement; Arrow of Light 4)

- Organize a special overnight campout just for the graduating boys and their dads. You could combine this with your ward's father/son campout in May to commemorate the restoration of the Aaronic priesthood. If Boy Scouts attend, then Webelos fufill requirements for Outdoorsman 4, 12. (Webelos Badge Requirement; Webelos Outdoorsman 1, 2, 3, 7, 8, 11; Arrow of Light 5)

- Invite your ward's scoutmaster to have a conference with your graduating boys. (Webelos Badge Requirement, Arrow of Light 6)

- Help the graduating boys learn the Boy Scout promise and prepare their uniforms for advancement. (Webelos Badge Requirement; Arrow of Light 7a, b, c)

9
Motivation and Recognition

Help the boys understand that the suggested tasks in their book are not "busy work," but that these tasks actually introduce them to things they will be doing for the rest of their lives: studying the scriptures, setting goals, learning, growing, and serving.

Every boy is unique and progresses at a different rate, so it's important for him to understand that the goals he selects are for him to improve himself and not to compete with others. In Cub Scouting, boys are judged against their own standard, not against other boys. "Do your best" is the Cub Scout Motto. Familiarize parents with the program and offer suggestions for them to support their son. Help the boys and their parents look at the activities they are already involved in and see how they can apply towards meeting some of the goals.

Once all of the requirements have been met, the Primary president and bishop (or branch president) sign the Faith in God certificate and recognize the child's accomplishments in Primary. Your bishop may also want to mention the award in Sacrament meeting. Boys should be working on some Scout achievements, electives, belt loops, and pins so that they can receive some form of recognition of progress at every monthly pack meeting. There are beads, patches, and pins of all kinds available to the Scouts. As they receive monthly recognition and a healthy dose of praise, they'll be more motivated to keep working hard.

In addition to the beads, patches, and pins that can be earned as the boys advance to a higher rank, there are also twenty-three sports activity areas and seventeen academic areas where the boys can earn belt loops and more pins! These additional awards can be earned any time. You should plan activities so that each month your boys will receive an award for something. Let the families of your boys know that these additional belt loops and pins can be earned outside of Scouts. You can purchase a book that lists all of the awards and their requirements or simply go online at www.boyscouttrail.com to see the lists for free! There is something for every boy's taste.

Academic Program:

Art	Collecting	Geology	Music
Astronomy	Communicating	Heritages	Science
Chess	Computers	Languages and cultures	Weather
Citizenship	Geography	Map and compass	Wildlife Conservation

Sports Program:

Archery	BB Gun Shooting	Badminton	Baseball
Basketball	Bicycling	Bowling	Fishing
Flag Football	Golf	Gymnastics	Ice Skating
Marbles	Physical Fitness	Roller Skating	Snow Ski and Board Sports
Soccer	Softball	Swimming	Table Tennis
Volleyball			

PRIMARILY FOR CUB SCOUTS

Webelos Scouts are busy earning various badges to prepare them for Boy Scouts, so the following list shows how some of the belt loops can be linked with requirements they might already be working on for rank advancement:

Earn This Academics Belt Loop	Get credit for this Webelos Activity Badge:
Art	Artist
Astronomy	Scientist
Chess	Scholar
Citizenship	Citizen
Communicating	Communicator
Computers	Communicator
Geography	Traveler
Geology	Geologist
Heritages	Family Member
Language and Culture	Scholar
Map and Compass	Traveler
Mathematics	Scholar or Engineer
Music	Showman
Science	Scientist
Weather	Scientist
Wildlife Conservation	Naturalist

MOTIVATION AND RECOGNITION

Earn this Sports Belt Loop	Get credit for this Webelos Activity Badge
Swimming	Aquanaut
Physical Fitness	Athlete
(all sports belt loops)	Sportsman

Other awards that are available to all Cub Scouts include:
Cub Scout Outdoor Activity Award
Emergency Preparedness Award
International Activity Badge
Interpreter's Strips
Leave No Trace Awareness Award
Recruiter Strip
Religious Emblems
Whittling Chip Card
World Conservation Award
National Summertime Award

Go online at www.usscouts.org to read the requirements for these special awards.

✦ Have a plaque made that can be hung on the wall by the bishop's office or in the Primary room for all to see the names of the boys who have received their Faith in God award.

✦ If your den or pack is planning an extra special event, you might consider designing an original patch that the boys can receive for their participation. Talk to your local Boy Scout Council for guidelines.

✦ Design special "B-Class" T-shirts for your den or pack that the boys can wear to special outings when a uniform might not be appropriate because it will get too muddy or dirty. Present the T-shirts as a reward for reaching a particular goal or even as a gift at baptism for the boys who turn eight and can now join your pack.

✦ Create a special tradition for recipients of the Arrow of Light Award, such as presenting them with a real arrow at a pack meeting, painting stripes on their face while explaining what each symbol of the Arrow of Light represents, designing a plaque that hangs in the Church building with the names of all the recipients, and so forth.

✦ Create a chart the boys can keep at home or use at Church that will keep them motivated each week. Encourage positive reinforcement rather than negative competition. Some samples can be found at www.sugardoodle.com and www.theideadoor.com. If you want to create a progress chart to display on the wall for everyone to see, you might consider having each boy make-up an alias name to protect their identity so that if they don't progress as quickly as the other boys they won't be embarrassed. (Wolf Elective 3a, e; Academic Belt Loop for Art)

✦ Set up a table at each pack meeting where all of the Cub Scouts can display items they've made during the month. They're sure to get lots of "oohs" and "aahs" from adoring parents.

✦ Present a larger version of the certificate in the back of the Faith in God book for them to frame and hang on their walls. A good one can be found at http://www.theideadoor.com/PDF%20Files/Primary/Faith%20in%20God/FIGboyscert.pdf. (Webelos Craftsman pin 1, 2, 3)

✦ Have the boys bring blankets, pillows, and their "Faith in God" books to a den or pack meeting. Make popcorn and watch a Church movie or play a game while the leaders pull one boy out at a time to update his Faith in God book and go over his goals.

✦ Have a monthly or quarterly P.I.E. night. Tell the boys P.I.E. stands for "Personal Interview Event" where each boy sits down with a leader and goes over

MOTIVATION AND RECOGNITION

his goals. While the other boys are waiting for their turn, they can bake and eat pies or work on a group project.

✦ Create a special binder for each boy to either keep at the den meeting location or to take home. (Be forewarned, however, that if he takes it home, you may never see it again!) Things you could include are a copy of the Faith in God booklet, copies of "The Living Christ" and "The Family: A Proclamation to the World," a pack list with phone numbers for the boys and the leaders, a monthly calendar, his Scout book, and notepaper.

✦ Include a Faith in God article in your ward or Primary newsletter to spotlight some of the boys' accomplishments. Include articles and artwork created by the boys.

✦ Each time a boy completes a task he earns a square of fabric that will become his very own quilt or quilted pillow. Have a big quilt-making party at the end of the year.

✦ Buy an oil lamp and have the boys drop some "oil" into the lamp each week if they have completed a project or worked on one. Talk about the parable of the ten virgins and their own spiritual preparation. The boys could each have their own lamp, or you could have one large one for all of the boys combined. Once the lamp is full you could choose to have a party or some other special reward.

✦ Present each boy with one piece of a Nativity set when he has finished a goal or at the end of each year's accomplishments. The completed set is something that will be cherished in his home as a young man and when he has his own family.

✦ Present the boy with a picture of him shaking hands with the stake president, bishop, or Primary president (or all of the above!) when he has completed all of the Faith in God goals.

✦ Make a Faith in God family home evening lesson to help family members understand the program and how they can support the Primary boy in their family. Choose goals they can work on together. See the large list of activities that can be done at home in this book and encourage parents to be proactive with their son's advancement. (Webelos Badge Requirement 8a, b, c, d, e)

✦ Encourage the Primary presidency to ask children to give talks on the Faith in God program and goals during sharing time on Sundays. (Webelos Badge Requirement 8a, b, c, d, e; Webelos Showman 1, 16)

✦ Have a weekly "Spotlight" moment each time you meet by shining a flashlight on each boy while he talks about his recent accomplishments in and out of Cub Scouts.

✦ Invite the boys to decorate a special container where they can put candy as they complete requirements. When the jar is full, present it to the bishop to put on the desk in his office for him to share with future visitors.

✦ Have a healthy competition between the boys and the leaders to see who can pass off the most goals within a certain period. The group that "wins" is treated to a special treat or event by the other group.

✦ Have the boys decorate a Primary bulletin board with Faith in God information.

✦ Write Faith in God goals on slips of paper and have the boys draw one out of a hat to decide which one they're going to do that day or, to allow you more preparation time, for the next den meeting.

✦ This particular tradition can be controversial for safety reasons, but fun if you get the okay from your ward leaders. When a Cub Scout earns the rank of Bobcat, have strong men hold him upside down while the mother pins his Bobcat pin on him. Once the boy stands up his pin will be upside down. He has to "Do a Good Turn" before he can turn his pin right side up. The moms may worry, but the boys will love it!

✦ When the boys finish a goal, put their names on a slip of paper in a jar. Once a month or quarter, draw a few names of winners to receive a special treat.

10

Parental Support

Parents have the responsibility to help their children learn and live the gospel. Primary leaders and teachers assist parents in this great responsibility. Some parents think it is the other way around. Help parents understand that your role as a Primary leader is to help them. If parents and leaders work together as a team, the children will be surrounded by love, support, guidance, and protection. Print out the list in the appendix at the end of the book that shows parents how many requirements they can do at home and encourage them to participate more in their son's success in the Cub Scout program.

Getting support from the parents of your Primary boys is extremely important for the progress and success of your program. When parents see that their son is being blessed by his attendance, they will be more eager to send him to den meetings, pack meetings, Church, and Activity Days. Parents will become supportive when they see that your activities and efforts are helping their son to strengthen their home and family!

LDS families have busy lives, and most likely, the parents are coordinating the activities of several children at the same time. When you communicate with the parents ahead of time of what you've planned for their son, they will better support your calendar with enthusiasm. Plan ahead, and be organized.

Invite the parents of all your boys to form a Scout Committee that will

PRIMARILY FOR CUB SCOUTS

help organize the big Scouting events, such as Day Camp, Blue and Gold Banquet, Pinewood Derby, and so forth. When you invite parents to help organize and carry out a special part in a den or pack meeting, they are more likely to attend! Participating in an event also helps parents see all of the hard work that goes into an activity, and they just might appreciate what you do more!

Here are a few ideas to get more support from the parents:

✦ Invite parents to join you every now and then for activities, and you'll pass off the requirement on page 9 of the "Faith in God" booklet!

✦ Send parents weekly emails with an updated calendar. They'll love it if you attach photos that were taken from last week's activity.

✦ Send them a monthly newsletter. It could be in email form or an actual hard copy. Have a summary of what happened during the month and a peek at next month's events. Have the boys help pick out a fun name such as "The Cub Hubbub" or "About Scouts." The newsletter doesn't have to be long, but if you include photos and praise for the boys' accomplishments, it's sure to be a hit!

✦ Find out what the parents' talents are and recruit them to teach classes or activities where they can share their skills with the boys.

✦ Make sure parents have a copy of the "Faith In God" booklet. Give them the list in this book of activities they're allowed to pass off with their son at home and encourage them to be proactive about their son's progress.

✦ Do in-home visits with their son to go over their son's progress. Most parents will be impressed that you care so much to give their son such personal attention. Visit his bedroom and let him tell you about his favorite things in his room. Let his parents hear you expressing interest in what he does.

✦ Honor parents at a special Parents Appreciation activity. Have the boys help plan the event so they can pass off requirements (Wolf Achievement 8c, e; Wolf Achievement 10b; Bear Achievement 15 a, b)

- Encourage the boys to write their parents thank-you letters. (Wolf Elective 21b; Bear Achievement 18b, e; Webelos Communicator 11, 13; Academic Belt Loop for Communicating)

- Encourage parents to complete the exercises with their son in the booklet "How to Protect Your Children from Child Abuse." Invite all families who have done this to enjoy a special ice cream sundae after a den meeting. (Bobcat Trail 8; Webelos Badge Requirement 1; Webelos Fitness pin 2)

- Always speak positively about the parents in front of the boys so they will see that you respect their families.

- Invite the parents to take turns bringing refreshments for den meetings, pack meetings, and other special occasions. If everyone contributes, then it's not a burden. Some parents really shine when it comes to refreshments, so this gives them an opportunity to use their creative talents!

- Write the parents a thank-you letter, expressing how much you appreciate all of the good things that they have taught their son.

- Call the parents and ask them what they think you could do to better touch their son's heart and help him want to live the gospel. They'll be grateful that someone cares enough to ask. Ask the parents how you can help them get their son to Church and activities on time if that is a problem.

- Invite parents to be guest speakers in a panel, addressing a topic of a particular interest or talent they have. Their son will beam with pride.

- Let parents know what goals you're emphasizing each month and include a list of things they could talk about and do with their son at home to reinforce what you are trying to accomplish.

- Have a look-alike contest, showcasing photos of the boys and their parents when they were babies.

- Have a family tree climbing activity where the boys can bring photos, pedigree charts, and other memorabilia to share what they know about their ancestors. If you invite the parents, they will be grateful for the opportunity to talk about the legacy their parents have left. (Webelos Family Member 1; Academic Belt Loop for Heritages)

✦ Involve the parents in a big craft project or something they can work on with their son during a big Workshop Weekend. See the list of craft ideas in Chapter 8. (Wolf Achievement 5e; Wolf Achievement 8e; Wolf Elective 3a, e)

✦ Ask parents to keep you informed of their son's special events such as piano recitals, sports events, competitions, performances, and other occasions you could attend to show you care.

✦ Encourage the parents to write a "love letter" to their son for a special occasion.

✦ Send each boy home with ideas for family home evening lessons, refreshments, games, and other activities for his family. (Wolf Achievement 10b, g)

✦ Create a special scrapbook for each boy. Add photos of him and other momentos during his time in Primary. He can even work on it with you. Present it to his parents when he graduates or at the end of each year. (Wolf Achievement 12e; Webelos Artist Badge 2)

✦ Help each boy recognize the unique challenges his family faces and talk about how he can be a blessing to his parents and family. (Wolf Achievement 10b, g)

✦ Have all of the children adopt one of the boy's families each month. The boys could write letters of appreciation, do a "heart attack," bring the family goodies, give them an award, help baby-sit, help them with yard work, or invite them to be the guests of honor at a special activity. (Webelos Handyman pin 1, 13; Academic Belt Loop for Communicating)

✦ Have a cooking contest and then create a special Primary cookbook with all of the entries. Each boy can choose his mom or dad to help so it's a team effort and contest. You can even throw in a family history twist to it by requiring that all recipes must be either a family favorite or one that has been passed down in their family. (Wolf Achievement 8e; Webelos Family Member 1; Academic Belt Loop for Heritages)

✦ Have a dessert social where Scout leaders introduce the program to pack parents, reviewing the material in the "Parent Guide" at the front of their son's book. Help them understand their role as "Akela."

✦ Write ideas for creative, fun family activities onto colored slips of paper and then put them into a decorated mason jar or a round cardboard oatmeal box. Have every boy create one for his own family to use. Talk about how the family who plays together stays together! Talk about other fun family traditions and ways to strengthen the family closeness and create special memories. (Wolf Achievement 10a; Wolf Elective 9 b, c)

✦ Encourage your bishopric to hold a special Parents Meeting on the fifth Sunday of the month, perhaps during the Sunday School hour or during a combined Relief Society and priesthood lesson that focuses on the Primary and how parents can support them. Familiarize parents with the Faith in God goal programs so parents can ask their children informed questions at home and celebrate their progress.

✦ Have the boys decorate a mat that will go around a framed copy of "The Family: A Proclamation to the World." (Wolf Achievement 10a; Wolf Elective 9b, c; Webelos Craftsman pin 1, 2, 3)

✦ Encourage the boys to seek a father's blessing, perhaps at the beginning of each school year. Work with home teachers when there is no priesthood holder in the home. Talk about the importance of doing well in school. (Webelos Scholar 2)

…11

Funtastic Traditions

Traditions create a feeling of unity and security. Some of the following ideas might not work in your ward or branch, but they may get you thinking about what special traditions can create continuity and wonderful memories in your Primary, Cub Scout den, and pack.

✦ Invite another ward or the entire stake to share a Faith in God activity together annually. It could include a craft, short lesson, refreshments, guest speaker, stations the boys rotate through to pass off various achievements, or a service project. (Wolf Elective 9a; Webelos Badge Requirement 8a, b, c, d, e; Webelos Badge Requirement 8e; Webelos Citizen Badge 8)

✦ Create special mailboxes for each boy. You could use an actual mailbox or assign a hanging file folder for each boy in a box. Put little notes, announcements for future events, and handouts in it. Open the mailbox at every meeting and pass out everyone's mail. At a quick glance the leaders can see whose folder is full and tell who hasn't been attending very much lately. The boys could also take turns being responsible for putting a surprise in the folders once a month. Keep some stationery and pens near the box to encourage the boys to write kind notes to each other. (Bear Elective 18b; Academic Belt Loop for Communicating)

✦ Make den flags that can be paraded into the room every time you have a pack meeting.

✦ Years ago, neckerchief slides were a big deal. Cub Scouts and Boy Scouts learned how to make all different kinds and for different occasions. Teach the boys how to make some out of a variety of material: felt, wood, cardboard, clay, and so forth. (Wolf Elective 3a, e; Webelos Artist pin 7; Academic Belt Loop for Art)

✦ In a world full of terrible news headlines, it's nice to hear some good news! Once a month, have the boys share with the den or pack some good news. It can be anything from getting an A on a test to scoring a goal in a soccer game. The boys can do some of the creative cheers listed in Chapter 24. If you have talkative boys who get easily distracted, you could set the timer for one minute for each boy. You could even make and use a "talking stick." Invite each boy to hold it while he's talking, which reminds the others that they need to be quiet until their turn.

✦ Take lots of photos of the boys at every activity so that at the end of each year you can present a special scrapbook for them, or you could make the scrapbooks together. (Webelos Artist Badge 2)

✦ Make Boy Scout clothes for a big teddy bear. Give him a name and make him your den or pack mascot. You could invite each den that passes off the most achievements to take the mascot home for the week.

✦ If your ward doesn't already participate in "Scout Sunday," begin the tradition! Cub Scouts and Boy Scouts are invited to wear their uniforms to Church, usually on a Sunday in February.

✦ Create a Cub Scout Choir. If you spend a few minutes singing each time you gather, you'll be able to polish a song fairly quickly that could then be sung as a musical number in Sacrament meeting, at a pack meeting, or even for sharing time. Try to incorporate the boys' instrumental talents as well. Webelos who discuss opera and musicals pass off Showman 1 and 22. Don't stress out over this idea—not all boys are into singing! (Wolf Elective 11a, b, c, d, e, f; Webelos Showman 1, 9, 11; Academic Belt Loop for Music)

PRIMARILY FOR CUB SCOUTS

✦ Begin a Primary newsletter. If your ward or Primary presidency isn't already creating a special newsletter, you could create your own. Present your boys with a newsletter monthly or quarterly. Include pictures of past activities, articles about the boys, fun polls, helpful information, announcements for upcoming events, poems the boys have written, suggestions for cool websites to check out, birthdays, leaders' phone numbers, and spotlights on boys who accomplish their goals or just need a little extra attention. Fill the pages with whatever interests your boys have and encourage them to submit their own artwork, stories, and photos. It doesn't have to be an enormous project; even a two-sided sheet of paper where you praise the boys would be great! Have a contest to see who can come up with the best title for the newsletter.

✦ Some packs have terrific annual traditions of holding a "Raingutter Regatta," "Space Derby," or "Model Rocket Mahem." If you don't have those traditions, start them! You'd be amazed at how many websites exist with instructions on how to carry out these events. (Bear Achievement 21a, b, f, g)

✦ Establish a "New to You" table. Set out a table where the boys could bring any of their unwanted items from home. Anyone is free to take whatever they want. The items that remain at the end of the activity could be delivered to Goodwill, Deseret Industries, Vietnam Vets, or any other organization of your choosing. You could also deliver items to your local special needs branch you have in your area. You can have the boys bring random items each month or designate a different theme each month such as toys, school supplies, clothing, and so forth. This could be a one-time activity or held every month.

✦ Set out a "S.O.S Table." S.O.S stands for "Seek Out Service." Each month or quarter, one or two organizations are spotlighted so the boys can get ideas for service projects that they can get involved in with their families. This is an opportunity to introduce the boys to ways they can become more involved in their community and reach out to others. You can provide pamphlets or flyers with a contact phone number so the boys can follow through with their interest. Organizations you might want to introduce to the boys could include:

American Kidney Foundation, Second Harvest, American Cancer Society, Candy Stripers, United Way, Toys for Tots, local nursing homes they can visit or perform in, local hospitals they can volunteer in, and so forth. If you plan to do a conservation service project with your den or pack, your boys will also meet requirements for the World Conservation Award, "Leave No Trace" Awareness Award, and for the Webelos Badge. (Webelos Badge Requirement 8e; Webelos Citizen 1b, c, 17)

✦ Control chitchat by creating a special time for it. The boys always have so much to say to one another each time they gather, and it's often frustrating to keep telling them to be quiet during the lesson. When you first get together, set the timer and allow the boys to chitchat as fast as they can until the timer goes off. Once they hear the bell, they know their time is up and now it's the leader's turn to talk.

✦ Establish "Gathering Time." Provide a Gathering Time activity at the beginning of their meetings as the children slowly meander into the room. It could be a craft, puzzle, writing assignment, or art project that gives the prompt arrivals something to do while waiting for the stragglers to join in.

✦ Put together a Primary photo directory. Digital cameras make putting together a photo directory a snap! The directory could include phone numbers, addresses, and email addresses of the boys and leaders. Although this idea encourages increased communication among all those in the Primary program, it could also be the source of security problems for the safety of your boys if placed in the wrong hands. You would need to stress the importance of the boys' safety before handing out such a list and would need to get parental permission beforehand.

✦ Door prizes are a fun way to reward positive behavior. For example, if your boys have a tendency to straggle in late every week, you could award door prizes to all the boys who are on time. If you want to encourage missionary work with the boys, you could offer a little prize to each boy who brings a friend each month. Door prizes could also be offered randomly to add a little excitement.

Prizes don't have to cost much and can even be donated by local vendors. All you have to do is ask! Organizations love donating things to Scouts.

✦ Present a Book of Mormon challenge. Each week or month challenge the boys to share a Book of Mormon with a non-member friend. Have the boys give a short report on their experiences. Have a contest to see who can give away the most copies. (Wolf 11a, b, c; Bear Achievement 1a, b)

✦ Have a "Scout Spotlight." Each month a different boy is spotlighted and given a little gift. He stands in front of the group while someone tells all about his favorite things, his accomplishments, talents, and why he is so special to the Cub Scout program in your ward. You could also tell the group all about him and have the others guess who they think it is and then present him to the group.

✦ A friendship "Cub Can" could be filled and presented each month to a boy whose name has been drawn out of a hat. The recipient then brings the specially decorated can filled with new items for the next month's "Cub Can" minute. The can tradition should not be a financial burden, but an opportunity to simply express friendship and Scout spirit.

✦ Serve a special cake once a month to celebrate all of the boys and leaders who have a birthday that month. You could also include birthdays of current apostles, past prophets, or other people in Church history. (Bear Achievement 1 a)

✦ Send "Monthly Missionary Messages." Set out a table at each pack meeting with stationery, note cards, markers, and so forth so that the boys can write letters of encouragement to the missionaries who are serving from the ward. All of the letters could then be mailed either separately or together in a special care package from the Cub Scouts or Primary. Similar packages of cards and letters could be mailed to any ward members serving in the military or college students away for the school year. (Bear Achievement 1a, b; Bear Achievement 18 b; Webelos Communicator 11; Academic Belt Loop for Communicating)

✦ Give the recipes for refreshments served during the month to the boys. To keep their growing collection in a safe place, give them a special binder or box where they can keep all of the recipes together. The boys could also submit their favorite family recipes to create a ward cookbook. (Bear Achievement 9a, b, e; Academic Belt Loop for Collecting)

✦ Set up a "Get to Know You" table. Once a year, invite the boys to bring a few items to put on a table at a pack meeting. This is a great way for the other boys to get to know them a little better.

✦ Everyone who rides with another boy to den meetings gets a little "Carpool Award" prize. Carpooling encourages the boys to bond, invite, and remind each other to attend, in addition to saving gas money and the environment!

✦ Create a "Lunch Bunch." Once a quarter, invite the Primary presidency and Scout leaders to meet for lunch with the boys at their school. Give an award for the "Most tasty brown bag" or other goofy categories.

✦ Have a countdown for the next temple that will be built and dedicated, especially if there is one near you. Do special activities to prepare or find pen pals from a ward or branch in that area you can write to. (Bear Achievement 18b; Webelos Communicator 11; Academic Belt Loop for Communicating)

✦ Begin an annual tradition called the "Crystal Apple" or "Teacher Appreciation Golden Apple." Each boy invites a teacher, coach, or adult who has made an impact on his life to a special dinner. This can be an annual event and really encourages reaching out into the community. (Wolf Elective 9a; Webelos Citizen 1b c, 13)

✦ Being extremely careful to protect the identities of your boys, you might consider creating a ward Cub Scout website. You could post announcements, maps, links, and so forth. You would need to get parental consent before posting any photos and never reveal addresses or phone numbers online. For free space, check out www.myfamily.com and www.homestead.com. (Academic Belt Loop for Map and Compass)

✦ Get together to watch a general conference session together. Play Conference Bingo. To help the boys prepare for Conference, you could also play "Name That Apostle" and teach the boys a little bit about each of the men in the Quorum of the Twelve. Another fun game to learn about the apostles is to play "FISHers of Men" (like Go Fish; collect four of the same pictures to make a "book"). Make playing cards by copying four pictures of each Apostle. No need to reinvent the wheel—you can find the cards online at www.lds.about.com.

✦ Hold a "Linger Longer." The Cub Scouts could begin a tradition in your ward to hold a monthly after-Church supper, complete with awards for best dishes. (Wolf Achievement 8c; Bear Achievement 9a, c, f)

✦ Award "Caught Being Good" coupons to boys when you want to reinforce good behavior (attendance, language, kindness, service). They can turn in their coupon to the bishop, who will have a special basket of treats waiting for them (which you provide him).

✦ Invite a "Sister Friendly" to attend your Cub Scout den meeting once a month or quarter to share stories or play games that incorporate the *Friend* magazine. With parental permission, take pictures of the boys or drawings the boys have made to submit to the magazine in the "Our Creative Friends" section. Show the boys how to make the recipes from the "Kitchen Krafts" section. You could also learn a song that has been printed in the *Friend* or do the mazes and games to get them excited about reading their issue at home. (Webelos Showman 1, 9, 11; Academic Belt Loop for Music)

✦ Invite the boys to participate in a contest to design a special patch for your ward. (Webelos Artist)

✦ Create a "Wish List" of items your den or pack would like to get donated, such as craft supplies, treasure box toys, party decorations, and so on. Pass the list around at Church or post it at www.freecycle.org.

12

Fun Field Trips

Before heading out the door with your well-behaved Cub Scouts, be sure parents sign a permission slip with emergency contact information you can keep in a binder. It's helpful to keep a list of parent's cell phone numbers in case you need to return later than originally planned or something unexpected happens. Don't be afraid to ask parents to help chaperone too.

Fun Field Trips
(Webelos who plan and go on almost any field trip can fulfill requirements for the Traveler pin.)

Airport—Bear Achievement 10a
Aquarium—Academic Belt Loop for Science
    Academic Belt Loop for Wildlife Conservation
Art Gallery—Bear Elective 9b
    Academic pin for Art
    Academic Belt Loop for Collecting
Aviary—Wolf Elective 13a, b, c, d, e, f
    Bear Achievement 5d
    Academic Belt Loop for Collecting
    Academic Belt Loop for Wildlife Conservation
Bank—Webelos Traveler 1, 2, 3, 4, 5, 6, 9, 10, 11

Beach or seashore—Bear 10a
    Academic Belt Loop for Wildlife Conservation
Bookstore—Wolf Elective 6 a, b, c
    Bear 8a
Campout—Wolf Elective 23a, b, c, d, g, h
    Bear 12a
    Webeleos Outdoorsman 1, 2, 3, 4, 5, 7, 8, 11, 12
    Academic Belt Loop for Wildlife Conservation
Concert—Wolf Achievement 10 f
Family Home Storage Center (Bishop's Storehouse)—Wolf Achievement
    6a, b, c
    Wolf Achievement 8a, b
    Wolf Achievement 11a, c, d
    Bear Achievement 13g
Farm or ranch—Bear Achievement 10a
    Academic Belt Loop for Wildlife Conservation
Fire Station—Wolf Elective 22d
    Webelos Readyman 11
Fishing—Wolf Elective 19a, b, c, d, e, f
    Academic Belt Loop for Wildlife Conservation
Forest or Christmas tree farm—Webelos Forester Badge
    Academic Belt Loop for Wildlife Conservation
Geological Site—Webelos Geologist pin
    Academic Belt Loop for Geology
    Academic Belt Loop for Wildlife Conservation
Government (state capitol)—Wolf Achievement 4f
Hike—Wolf Achievement 10c
    Bear Achievement 12b
    Webelos Badge Requirement
    Arrow of Light 5
    Webelos Outdoorsman 9 (if the hike is 3 miles)

Academic Belt Loop for Wildlife Conservation
Historic Place—Wolf Achievement 4 f
>Bear Achievement 3c, d

Library—Wolf Elective 6a, b, c
>Bear Achievement 8a
>Webelos Communicator 6

Museum—Wolf Achievement 10c
>Bear Achievement 10a
>Bear Elective 9b
>Academic Belt Loop for Art
>Academic Belt Loop for Collecting
>Academic Belt Loop for Science
>Academic Belt Loop for Wildlife Conservation

Nature Center (Botannical garden, agricultural exhibition) —
>Wolf Elective 15e
>Webelos Naturalist Badge 1a, b, c, 4, 6, 7, 8, 9, 10, 11
>World Conservation Award
>Webelos who draw or paint an outdoor picture fulfill Webelos Artist 3
>Academic Belt Loop for Science
>Academic Belt Loop for Wildlife Conservation

Newspaper Office—Bear Achievement 8a
>Bear Achievement 17c
>Webelos Communicator 7

Park—Wolf Achievement 1a, b, c, d, e, f, g, j, k, l
>Wolf Achievement 2e, f
>Wolf Achievement 10c
>Wolf Elective 18a, b, e
>Bear Achievement 10a
>Bear Elective 9c
>Academic Belt Loop for Wildlife Conservation

Primarily for Cub Scouts

Picnic—Bear Achievement 12c
Planetarium—Bear Elective 1c
    Academic Belt Loop for Astronomy
    Academic Belt Loop for Science
Play (Theater)—Wolf Achievement 10f
    Webelos Showman 1, 17, 20, 22
Police Station—Wolf Elective 22d
    Bear 7a, b, d, e, f
    Webelos Citizen pin 9
Radio Station—Webelos Communicator 7, 16
Recycling Center—Wolf Achievement 7c, d
    Bear Achievement 6a, c
    Academic Belt Loop for Wildlife Conservation
Red Cross Center—Wolf Achievement 3c
    Wolf Elective 16c
    Webelos Readyman 2, 3, 4, 5, 6, 7, 15
Rock Climbing—Webelos Geologist pin 1, 2, 3, 4, 6, 8
    Academic Belt Loop for Geology
    Skate park or Skate store—Webelos Handyman pin 9
TV Station—Bear Achievement 17c
    Webelos Communicator 7, 16
    Academic Belt Loop for Weather
Walk—Wolf Achievement 10c
    Webelos Athlete pin 5e
Wildlife Refuge or Game Preserve—Bear Achievement 5d
    Webelos Naturalist pin 1a, b, c, 4, 7, 8, 9, 10, 11
    Academic Belt Loop for Science
    Academic Belt Loop for Wildlife Conservation
Zoo—Webelos Naturalist pin 1a, b, c, 4, 6, 7, 8, 9, 10, 11
    Academic Belt Loop for Science
    Academic Belt Loop for Wildlife Conservation

13
Den Meeting Do's

Try to include the following elements in each of your den meetings:

1. Gathering activity—something for boys to do while waiting for everyone else to arrive. It could be a quiet activity or craft, but usually the boys arrive excited and with a lot of energy, so something more active and physical helps them get it out of their system and be able to focus when you're ready to start the meeting officially. Set out puzzles, crafts, paper, and markers to draw pictures or write letters to the missionaries, blocks of wood for nail pounding, and so forth. Websites that have plenty of ideas for gathering games and mixers are:
    www.gameskidsplay.net/
    www.funattic.com
    www.funandgames.org
    www.teach-nology.com/ideas/ice_breakers/
(Webelos Commnicator 3, 8, Academic Belt Loop for Communicating)

2. Opening Ceremony with the Cub Scout promise recited, opening prayer, song, and flag ceremony. Provide leadership opportunities for the boys to conduct.

Primarily for Cub Scouts

3. Announcements (keep them brief or you'll lose their attention!)
4. "Sharing Time" when the boys can talk or be spotlighted. You could have a "Missionary Moment," friendship can, "Good News" minute, awards, or some other fun tradition (see chapter 12 for ideas)
5. Short lesson that includes a Cub Scout Character Connection from the manual
6. Short lesson that includes an activity to fulfill a Duty to God requirement
7. Craft that fulfills a Scout requirement
8. Game or activity that fulfills a Scout requirement
9. Closing Ceremony that helps boys to summarize what they learned and includes a prayer
10. Refreshments

✦ Have a uniform inspection each week and be sure to wear your leader Scout shirt! Female Scout leaders are invited to wear either a yellow or tan Scout shirt. You could have a fun contest by wearing your uniform incorrectly every now and then to see which boys can guess what is wrong. (Webelos Badge requirement)

✦ Practice doing a flag ceremony each week so the boys will be comfortable doing it when it's their turn to present the flag during pack meeting. Say the Pledge of Allegiance to fulfill Wolf Achievement 2a. (Wolf Achievement 2a, b, c, d, e, f, g; Bear Achievement 3f, h, i; Webelos Badge Requirement 6; Webelos Citizen pin 3, 4, 5)

✦ Ask one of the boys to serve as a Denner each month so he can pass off Bear Achievement 24b.

Den Meeting Do's

✦ Create crossword puzzles that include words or ideas you'll be using in your den meeting. You can even have the boys design their own at www.puzzle-maker.com or www.armoredpenguin.com/crossword/. You can also put together fun anagrams very quickly at www.easypeasy.com/anagrams/. (Webelos Communicator 3, 12)

✦ Get a copy of the "Program Helps" guidebook from your local Scout store or online at www.boyscouttrail.com. It outlines the entire year's worth of themes for you and your pack. You can find all kinds of ideas for each month as well as a helpful list of requirements. There is no need to wrack your brain when it's all organized so well already!

✦ Attend your local Cub Scout Round Table where you will meet other leaders in your Council who are excited to share ideas. Someone from your ward should represent your pack each month, but oftentimes this assignment is forgotten. It's a great opportunity to do missionary work too, as most of the other leaders are often not members of the Church. You'll return home with renewed vigor and effective tools to use to strengthen your den and pack. A helpful website to visit is www.cub-roundtable.com.

✦ Visit websites that other packs have created to see photos and ideas that have worked for them. Do a Google search online for "Cub Scout Pack" and you'll be directed to dozens of good sites.

✦ A helpful outline for planning your den meetings can be found at www.pack414.org/denmeeting.doc.

14

Blue and Gold Banquet Brainstorm

The Blue and Gold Banquet is an annual tradition for families to get together with their Scout sons at an event that is a little bit different than the regular pack meeting. Some wards hold fancy banquets, but it could also be as simple as an outdoor picnic or potluck affair. Traditionally, the Blue and Gold Banquet is held in February to celebrate the anniversary of the Boy Scout program in February 1910. The Cub Scout organization was created twenty years later.

A Scout committee should be organized to help plan events such as this one and could include Scout parents or other adults. Encourage your bishop and Primary presidency to provide a helpful committee so that den leaders are not overwhelmed. The committee should select a theme several months in advance. Each Cub Scout den could work on decorations, seating arrangements, invitations, and table decorations weeks before the event. You can find some cute craft ideas at http://crafts.kaboose.com/cub-scout/blue-gold/blue-and-gold-banquet-ideas.html. It includes instructions for nut and candy cups, blue and gold ribbon place mats, blue and gold banquet pins for each guest to wear, and other decorations.

Besides the dinner, the evening should include the following:

✦ Gathering activity for boys to do while families arrive or a mixer activity to get people to mingle
✦ Awards
✦ Special entertainment

BLUE AND GOLD BANQUET BRAINSTORM

- Skits performed by the boys
- Recognition and thanks to Scout leaders
- Short speech by sponsoring organization (the Church)
- Short speech by Scout Council or District leader (Be sure to invite them)
- Short speech reviewing the history of the Cub Scouts or how the program works
- Songs and audience participation activities
- Short announcements
- Flag ceremony
- Opening and closing prayers
- Great food! (Fancy doesn't necessarily equate "great" in a Cub Scout's mind.)

Talk to your ward activity leader for ideas on decorations, table settings, centerpieces, and room décor. She will likely have tons of resources and helpful advice. The list of themes is endless! This event should be fun and stress-free for families. You could even include a moment where families share how the Cub Scout program has blessed their families. Because this event is to celebrate the Cub Scout's birthday, you could simply plan a party with cake and ice cream, and include party games and the other elements listed above. Families should return home feeling grateful for Cub Scouts and excited to continue with renewed dedication to its goals.

Some packs give keepsake items to each guest. The boys can make a simple craft in their dens before the party. Think about presenting each den leader with a small thank-you gift as well. Some packs pay professional entertainers for the Blue and Gold Banquet, but you don't have to spend a lot of money. Talk to other packs in your area at your monthly roundtable meetings and see what they recommend. Maybe your local high school performing groups can entertain the Scouts for free. Check out the chapter on in this book on websites where you'll find a list of resources for more ideas.

15
Pinewood Derby

The Pinewood Derby is a great tradition. Volumes have been written about the Pinewood Derby with exhausting details on how to run one and how to win one. Elaborate software programs have also been written to help you organize heats, determine winners, and even create certificates. Your ward might consider investing in one of them, although some are quite pricey. According to the Church's budget guidelines, a fundraiser is allowed in order to purchase necessary equipment for Scouts. Some recommended programs are

www.microwizard.com
www.pinewood-derby-timer.com
www.newdirections.ws/
www.iawinner.com
www.etekgadget.com
www.awana.org
grandprix-software-central.com/gprm
www.pinewoodorganizer.com

The pinewood derby can be an emotional event, but if carried out properly, everyone can return home with a smile on their face. The boys spend quite a bit of time preparing their masterpieces for this big event, and they want to enjoy racing their car as many times as possible, so allow time for the boys to play on the track either before or after the official heats.

One of the best traditions I've ever seen is to hold an "Open Category" where anyone can race, including eager siblings and parents! Another fun category to hold races is "Anything Goes"—any car that fits on the track without damaging it is allowed to compete. The boys will get very creative and look forward to this event almost more than the regular race.

Because the pinewood derby tends to run long, be sure to provide other activities on the edges of the room to keep little ones from getting antsy, such as coloring pages, making cars out of edible ingredients or Legos, or a cookie-decorating station.

The boys and their siblings tend to get overly anxious about watching the heats, so rope off a restricted area with racing car flags to protect the track and eager fingers. Even then, you'll have to remind them several times not to step past the rope.

Help the boys build a stand to display their pinewood derby cars on. (Webelos Craftsman pin 1, 2, 3; Webelos Handyman pin 12, 14, 15, 16, 17)

Put a big box around each boy, gluing paper plates on the sides for wheels. Have a relay race with the boys in their "cars." Each "driver" goes to various stations where he eats licorice for fuel, gets water squirted in his face, and so forth.

If you have a large pack, consider staggering the starting times by Scout ranks. For example, the Wolves could start at 6:00, the Bears at 6:20, the Webelos at 6:40, and an awards ceremony at 7:00. That way families could arrive closer to their son's race time and not get bored waiting so long.

PRIMARILY FOR CUB SCOUTS

Some great web sites with helpful advice on rules, speed tips, and decorations for the event are:

www.maximum-velocity.com
www.abc-pinewood-derby.com
www.pinewoodextreme.com
www.pinewoodpro.com
www.winderby.com

16

Silly Cheers, Skits, and Songs

You can't be in Cub Scouts very long before you'll be expected to sing a song, lead some cheers, or plan a silly skit to be performed in front of the entire pack and their families. Not to worry. There are oodles of ideas online. All you need is a printer and some willing boys. Cub Scouts especially love songs, skits, and cheers with goofy actions, gross or weird lyrics, and wacky humor. There's a ham in every boy.

Cheers

Be generous with your praise when the boys accomplish something. There is always an excuse to celebrate and lead a cheer. Cub Scouts love crazy cheers in the place of applause. Here are just a few silly ones that are always a hit. They'll get your own creative juices flowing. Ask the boys to come up with some, and you'll be impressed with how clever they can be. Fill a special bucket or even an empty "Cheer" laundry detergent box with slips of paper where the following cheers are written. The Cub Master can choose a boy who will select a paper out of the bucket and lead the cheer or invent one of his own.

+ "Let's give a big hand to. . ."— Hold out an open palm towards the person

+ "Let's give a seal of approval to. . ."— Put your elbows together, and open and close your forearms and hands while barking like a seal in a high-pitched "Arf!"

Primarily for Cub Scouts

- The Mosquito Clap—Rapidly slap your face, neck, shoulders

- The Flea applause—Raise your hands above your head and applaud by clicking the nails of the thumb and forefinger on each hand.

- Tracting Missionary applause—Point your index finger and shout "Ding Dong!"

- Rainstorm Cheer—Start clapping your index finger against your opposite palm. Then add 2 fingers, then 3, 4, 5, and then back down to 1 again.

- Water sprinkler applause—Make a fist with the thumb sticking out and place the thumb on the end of your nose. Rapidly open and close your fist while making the sound of a sprinkler "Ch, Ch, Ch, Ch" and spin around as you go. After a complete circle, spin back the opposite direction saying "Wheee!"

- Jackhammer applause—Hold a pretend jackhammer with both hands while shouting "Bap-bap-bap-bap-bap!"

- Doctor's applause—Everyone opens their mouths and says "AAAAH!"

- Car applause—Make the motion of turning a key in the ignition and the sound of the car turning on. End with a screeching sound for stepping on the brakes.

- Clams—Put your palms together and keep the heels of your hands together while you clap.

- Silent Clap—Fake a clap but miss at the last moment

- Balloon Cheer—Make a fist and put your thumb in your mouth. Slowly open your fingers while blowing to resemble an enlarging balloon. Then flip out your hand and yell "Pop!"

- Cub Scout—Explain that when you call "Cub" or "Scout" the group is supposed to respond with the opposite word. Mix them up and speed it up for more fun.

- Hammer Cheer—Hold an imaginary nail in one hand and pretend to pound a hammer on it while saying, "Bang, Bang, Bang, Ouch!"

- Train applause—Make your hands move like wheels while quietly saying, "Chug-Chug-Chug-Chug." Slowly get louder and then pull an imaginary whistle while shouting "Whoo Whoo!"

- Motorcycle cheer—Hold your hands like you're gripping handlebars. Raise a foot and kick downward three times while making sputtering sounds. End with the engine starting and yell "Varoom!"

- Magician's applause—Everyone pretends to take off a top hat, reaches into the hat, and pulls out a rabbit as they say "Ta Daaaaa!"

- Bullfighter applause—Pretend to move a cape as if fighting a bull and shout "Ole!"

And the all-time most popular cheer is . . .

- The falling raindrop—Everyone sits on the floor holding their knees up close to their chest and yells, "AAAAAH!" as if the raindrop is falling through the sky. End by spreading your arms and legs flat on the ground and yell, "Splat!"

More fun cheers can be found online at:

www.scoutingpages.org
www.usscouts.org/macscouter
www.scouter.com
www.macscouter.com

Songs and Skits

One of the very best websites for song and skit ideas is www.macscouter.com. You can spend hours online reading through samples. Some are definitely better than others. Test some out on your boys during den meetings, and use the best ones at your pack meetings. No doubt they'll make you feel like a goofy kid again! Any time you teach your den a song you'll be fulfilling requirements for the Academic Belt Loop for Music!

Oftentimes, your scouts will get shy in front of an audience, making it difficult to hear what they're saying in the skit. If you have especially quiet boys (yeah, right!), you might try this effective technique: The adult leader reads the narration of the skit while the boys simply act out the parts.

Skits are usually goofy and fun, but try to slip in a moral to the story when possible and point out to the audience afterwards that the underlying lesson in the skit was a particular "Character Connection" from the Scout book or something from the Faith in God program.

The boys also enjoy watching their leaders do skits, so every now and then have all of the den leaders put together something fun and special. The boys absolutely love to see their leaders act crazy. You could also invite your bishopric, Primary presidency, or the missionaries to join in on a silly skit. Playful leaders are very endearing to both the scouts and to their parents. Have fun!

17

Pack Meeting Ideas

Pack meetings should occur every month and include each Cub Scout's family members. It should be a time of celebration and fun, as well as an opportunity to provide lots of praise for the boys' accomplishments in front of their adoring parents. Each pack meeting should include the following elements:

- Gathering activity for boys to do while families arrive
- Opening Prayer and song
- Flag Ceremony
- Announcements
- Introduction of new Scouts
- Uniform check
- Awards
- Skits performed by the boys
- Songs and audience participation activities
- Game or some kind of activty
- Craft or service project
- Closing prayer
- Closing flag ceremony
- Refreshments

The Cub Master should host the evening and be spontaneous with cheers, humor, and enthusiasm. A Scout Committee should be called to help him plan each month's pack meeting. Den leaders should be told a few weeks in advance what the theme will be so they can prepare their boys to provide appropriate skits, their craft items or projects for a display table, flag ceremony, and so forth.

A good rule of thumb is to keep your pack meeting no longer than one hour. Families are insanely busy, but if they know your event will only take an hour, they'll be grateful and more willing to attend. Plan activities for the whole family to participate in rather than focusing on the boys and throwing the bored parents in the back of the room. It should be a time for families to mingle and get to know one another each month.

It's helpful to create a special bulletin board in your church building where you can post announcements, sign-ups, and flyers that advertise upcoming pack meetings. List some of the fun activities that the boys and families can look forward to, and you're sure to see increased attendance. Get email addresses of each family in your pack so you can also send out weekly or monthly emails to remind them of upcoming activities. Remember to submit pack meeting announcements to the people in your ward who create the Sunday bulletin and the ward newsletter, if you have one. Make all of your announcements fun, so that others wished they were Cub Scouts too!

A fun way to involve entire families is to create an audience participation skit that matches your monthly theme. When you write a script, be sure to plug in the sound effects at the end of the sentence, otherwise the audience will make so much noise they won't hear the end of the phrase. Divide families into groups and have them stand up when their part is spotlighted. Throw a goofy costume on your Cub Master as he leads the story and you're sure to have a hit! Below is an example:

The Legend of Gold Nugget Gulch

Prospectors: "Eureeka!"
Pack Mules: (snort)
Gold Nuggets: "Cha-ching!"
Camp Cook: "Grubs on!"
Clementine: "Oh, my!"
Rattlesnakes: "Hisssssss"
Cactus: "Yucca, Yucca"
Bandits: "Boooo!"

Are you listless, tired, out of sort? Do you need excitement and some thrills? Then gather round and I'll tell you the story of Gold Nugget Gulch. You'll slap your knees and say "By doggie, that just cain't be true!" but I'll swear on my old grandpappy's britches it is!

How well I remember one night at the old gold mining town near the river where, gathered around a campfire, were a bunch of tired, but hopeful **PROSPECTORS**. The moon shone brightly, but not nearly as much as what was in their pockets: a few **GOLD NUGGETS**. Tied up to some trees nearby were the **PACK MULES**. Down by the river, washing the pots and pans from the evening's dinner, was the **CAMP COOK**. Off in the distance you could hear some **RATTLESNAKES**. A few tumbleweeds blew by and landed near a **CACTUS**.

At the edge of town crept some **BANDITS**. They had nothing but trouble on their minds. What they wanted was to steal a bunch of **GOLD NUGGETS**. They were scheming up a dreadful plan to get them. All they would have to do was kidnap one very important person: darling **CLEMENTINE**! Every man in town was in love with her, especially all of the **PROSPECTORS**. They'd be willing to do anything to rescue her, like trade her for all of their **GOLD NUGGETS**.

And so, around the corner tippy-toed the mean, ole **BANDITS**. Ever so quietly they snuck up to the house where sleeping inside was **CLEMENTINE**. With hardly a sound they grabbed her, tied her up and threw her on to one of their **PACK MULES**. She tried to scream, but no one could hear her over the sound of the **RATTLESNAKES**. (Try it again **RATTLESNAKES**, they were really loud!) Oh my darlin, oh my darlin, oh my darlin **CLEMENTINE**. What ever will she do?

They hadn't gone very far when suddenly a brilliant idea popped into the mind of our darling **CLEMENTINE**. She sank her teeth into the arm of the mean ole **BANDIT**. He was so surprised that he kicked his spurs into the poor **PACK MULE**. The frightened animal jumped and started running around all the other **PACK MULES**. It caused such a stir among all of the other **BANDITS** that they bumped into each other and landed on some **CACTUS**. She had tried to escape but even quicker than her were the **BANDITS**. They caught her again and tied her up.

Amazingly enough, at this exact time there was one other person in town who had heard her cries for help: the **CAMP COOK**! Thinking quickly he called over to get some help from the **PROSPECTORS**. They came running, although one of them tore his britches on a **CACTUS**. They grabbed all the pots and pans that had just been scrubbed sparkling, clean by the **CAMP COOK**. They had a plan to save **CLEMENTINE**. Working fast they began to spray paint the pots and pans so they would look like **GOLD NUGGETS**. See, now I told you would think this story isn't true! Stay with me, folks, the plot thickens here. They knew they could trick the greedy and foolish **BANDITS**.

Coming closer and closer to the miners' camp you could see the **BANDITS**. They were riding on their **PACK MULES** and had the beautiful prisoner with them: **CLEMENTINE**. As they moved closer one of them tripped over a **CACTUS**. Now, more angry than ever, the greedy villain shouted,

"Here's **CLEMENTINE**! We'll give her to you if you hand over all of your **GOLD NUGGETS**!" "We will!" shouted back the **PROSPECTORS**. They tossed over the pots and pans that had been spray painted to look like **GOLD NUGGETS**. The bad guys couldn't believe how huge they were and decided they wanted even more. They demanded to know where the huge treasures had been found by the **PROSPECTORS**.

The miners, Forty-niners, knew that these bad men were not only greedy, but were also foolish, and so they led the way to a cliff overlooking a deep canyon, called a gulch. Thinking about their dreams of being rich forever, the beautiful prisoner was released by the **BANDITS**. They looked over the edge to see the huge **GOLD NUGGETS**. Before the **BANDITS** knew what was happening, the quick-thinking **PROSPECTORS** pushed them over the edge. The miners tossed over the spray-painted pots and bonked the bad guys on their heads, making them fall all the way to the bottom. One of the pots landed on a **CACTUS**. Another landed on a **RATTLESNAKE**. "You're my heros!" exclaimed **CLEMENTINE**. "Oh my darlin', oh my darlin'," shouted the **CAMP COOK**.

For years people use to say that in that canyon there were still huge **GOLD NUGGETS**.

But you and I know better, it was just fool's gold! But that's not the end of the story. Two missionaries walked through the town and met the smart **PROSPECTORS**. The missionaries taught them about a book of gold, and after getting baptized, they all lived happily ever after!

-The End-

18

The Religious Square Knot Award

"**A** Scout is reverent." Scouts demonstrate reverence by being faithful in their duty to God. The Faith in God Award is different than Cub Scouting's Religious Square Knot award; however, they can go hand in hand. Requirements for the Boy Scouts of America "Youth Religious Emblem Award" satisfy some of the requirements for the Faith in God Award.

For each faith, a specific set of requirements is published and is established by the religious faith and not by the Boy Scouts of America. Most religions have their own requirements for earning this special award listed online at http://usscouts.org/scoutduty/index.html.

The award is a little purple patch with a white square knot on it. (Years ago the Church gave the boys a special pin to wear in addition to the patch, but they have been discontinued.) Once earned, the award is usually presented by the Church during sacrament meeting or Primary sharing time. Talk with your bishop to see how and where he would like to present this award. Cub Scouts may continue to wear their religious knot patch on their Boy Scout uniforms.

On the next page is a list of the seven requirements for Cub Scout members of The Church of Jesus Christ of Latter-day Saints to earn the religious square knot.

The Religious Square Knot Award

1. Give a family home evening lesson on Joseph Smith's First Vision (see Joseph Smith History 1:1–20). Discuss how Heavenly Father answers our sincere prayers.	Learning and Living the Gospel Faith in God booklet, pages 6–7	Wolf-Achievement 11 (page 94) Wolf Elective 22c Bear-Achievement 1a (page 27) Webelo's "Family Member" 5 (page 227) Communicating belt loop requirement #1
2. Give an opening and a closing prayer in family home evening or at Primary. Share your feelings about how prayer protects us and helps us to stay close to Heavenly Father and the Savior.	Learning and Living the Gospel Faith in God booklet, pages 6–7	Wolf-Achievement 11 (page 94) Part of Bear Achievement 1 (page 26) Webelo's Family Member 5 (page 227)
3. Tell a story from the Book of Mormon that teaches about faith in Jesus Christ. Share your testimony of the Savior.	Learning and Living the Gospel Faith in God booklet, pages 6–7	Wolf-Arrow point 22c (page 220) Part of the Communicating belt loop requirements

Primarily for Cub Scouts

4. Prepare a pedigree chart with your name and your parents' and grandparents' names. Prepare a family group record for your family and share a family story. Discuss how performing temple work blesses families.	Learning and Living the Gospel Faith in God booklet, pages 6–7	Heritage belt loop Bear-Achievement 8d (page 76) Webelo's "Family Member" (page 227) Wolf-Achievement 11 (page 94)
5. Write a letter to a teacher, your parents, or your grandparents telling them what you appreciate and respect about them.	Serving Others Faith in God booklet, page 9	Part of Communicating belt loop requirements Webelo's "Communicator" (page 165) Bear- Achievement 18b, 18e, 24d(pages 141, 143, 176)
6. Help your Primary leaders plan and carry out an upcoming quarterly activity.	Serving Others Faith in God booklet, page 9	Wolf-Arrow point 9a (page 152) Bear-Achievement 24c (page 176) If the Primary activity is a service project, this can also be part of the Citizenship belt loop requirements

7. Write a story, poem, or short play that teaches a principle of the gospel or is about Heavenly Father's creations.	Developing Talents Faith in God booklet, page 10	Webelo's "Communicator" (page 165) Bear-Achievement 18f (page 144) Wolf-Achievement 11 (page 94) Part of Communicating Pin requirements

Appendix 1:
Website Resources

Finding new ideas for Cub Scouts can be as easy as a click! A word of caution, however, about doing Internet searches for ideas: if you enter "Boys" into a search engine, you could get suggestions for links to all kinds of horrible pornographic websites. You must type in LDS, Primary, Activity Days, or Cub Scouts and even then, look at the description of the site before you click on it! Once you innocently click onto a porn site, they will have captured your computer information and will send you disgusting emails until you have to shut down your account! Unfortunately, I speak from experience.

LDS Web Sites with Scouting Ideas

www.lds.org The official web site of the Church of Jesus Christ of Latter-day Saints. Click on "Serving in the Church" then choose "Primary" and then "Primary Activity Days." This should be your first stop on the Internet!

www.ldscatalog.com Purchase official Church items

www.mormonscouting.com Ideas, clip art, games, skits for Boy Scouts that could easily be tweaked for Cub Scouts

www.ldsactivitydays.com Tons of fun ideas shared by many other Primary workers

http://latter-dayvillage.com Paid membership is required to access all of their very good resources

www.theideadoor.com/Primary.html Tons of fun ideas, clip art, charts

Appendix 1

www.christysclipart.com Free clip art for every occasion

www.sugardoodle.net Cute ideas for lessons, forum

www.ldssplash.com/callings/activity_days/activity_days.htm Some Primary ideas, but many more in other categories that could be adapted for Cub Scouts

www.jennysmith.net Wonderful resource for everything!

http://youngwomen.faithweb.com Has a helpful Primary page

http://lds.about.com/od/ldsprimary/ Lesson ideas, games, puzzles, word searches, downloads

www.eprimary.dk/index_uk.htm Games, downloads, clip art, lessons, music and more!

http://of-worth.com/cc/ Poetry, stories, quotes, ideas

http://www.mormonchic.com/gospel/achievement.asp Ideas based on the Achievement Days program

www.achievementdays.com Tons of ideas based on the Achievement Days program

www.ldsfiles.com/dir/Church_Organizations/Primary Tons of links, resources

www.lightplanet.com/mormons/primary/index.htm Overall Primary ideas, activity ideas based on the Achievement Days program

www.ldstoday.com/home/level2/PrimaryIdeas.php Overall Primary ideas

www.bellaonline.com/subjects/1992.asp Links to ideas for children

www.debanae.net Mostly Young Women things, but some free Primary clip art and products

LDS Search Engines

http://lds.mycityport.com
www.ldsindex.org/resources
www.ldslibrary.com
www.ldsabout.com
www.mormon-lds-gateway.org

www.ldstoday.com
www.mormonlinks.com
www.mormonfind.com
www.ldsvoices.com
http://www.mormonhaven.com/miscel.htm

APPENDIX I

Scout Websites • • • • • • 🐾

There are a few official Boy Scouts of America web sites and about a gazillion other sites created by enthusiastic Scout leaders. Someone out there has already asked the same question you have right now or has already planned the activity you're thinking about doing. Do a Google search for "Cub Scouts" and you'll see all kinds of websites created by individual packs as well.

www.scoutsoft.net FREE software to track Scouting and Faith in God progress, board games

www.scouting.org Official National Council of Scouts, forms, handbooks, online games the boys will get a kick out of!

www.usscouts.org/scoutduty/sd2gc33.html Information on LDS religious award for Cubs

www.bbpsoftware.co.uk Free downloadable scout games

Educational Web Sites

www.cubmaster.org
www.boyscouttrail.com
www.usscouts.org
www.scoutingmagazine.org
www.scoutcamp.org
www.jambo.org
www.worldscouting.org
www.macscouter.com
www.scoutmaster.org
www.cubpack81.com www.scouting-bsa.org
www.scouting.org
www.scouter.com
www.scoutstuff.org
www.lastfrontiercouncil.org
http://usscouts.org

www.edhelper.com/bingo.htm Build your own puzzles, worksheets and games

http:///www.familyfun.com Great magazine with tons of ideas for children and families.

http://www.debanae.net/ Ideas, clip art

www.homeandholidays.com recipes, crafts, patterns, miscellaneous ideas

www.dltk-holidays.com Tons of fun holiday ideas and celebrations you've never heard of with crafts and activities

www.kidsites.com Links to sites young kids love

Appendix I

Craft Ideas

Below are web sites with zillions of project ideas you could tweak to fit a gospel context.

www.makingfriends.com
www.creativekidsathome.com
http://gsleaders.org/files/crafts.htm
www.allcrafts.net/kids.htm
http://parentingteens.about.com/od/crafts/
http://craftsforkids.miningco.com/library/bltrashtr.htm
http://rubyglen.com/crafts.htm
www.geocities.com/Athens/1850/
www.fibrecraft.com
www.deltacrafts.com
www.childfun.com
www.achildswork.com

Merchandise

www.ldscatalog.com Order Church materials
www.scoutingbooks.com Helpful manuals and idea books
www.littlestreamrecords.com Primary songs and more
www.ldsfiles.com/link/?1024689378 LDS games, puzzles, teaching tools
www.brownbaggifts.com Gift ideas
www.jeannigould.com Beautiful LDS music
www.1on1.net tons of stuff
www.softlore.com memorizing scriptures software
www.ldsaudio.com LDS music, books
www.marvingoldstein.com/SBChildren%27sSongbook.htm Piano solo arrangements of Primary songs by the beloved Marvin Goldstein
www.orientaltrading.com Inexpensive and fun items for any occasion
http://www.lds-yw.com/ Primary stickers
www.byubookstore.com Tons of everything!
www.ldsliving.com LDS magazine
www.deseretbook.com LDS books, music, merchandise
www.seagullbooks.com LDS books, music, merchandise
www.ctr-ring.com CTR rings
www.cedarfort.com Lots of books, gift ideas, and merchandise

Appendix 1

Blogs

A blog is a type of online journal where people record their thoughts, experiences, and ideas on a specific subject. You can get some terrific ideas from people who have been in the trenches and know what works and what doesn't. The following are blogs written by people who really really love Scouts!

happyjellybeans.blogspot.com
www.thecubscoutleader.blogspot.com
www.primary-teacher-uk.co.uk
www.boyscouttrail.com/blog.asp
www.melrosetroop68.org/blog.html
wordpress.com/tag/cub-scouts/

Cub Scout Podcasts

A podcast is a recorded interview you can access any time of day or night on the Internet. It can also be downloaded for you to use on your mp3 player. You'll find that people who are really into the Scouting program absolutely love to share their wisdom and experiences! Here are just a few, among many, to get you started.

"The Leader's Campfire" www.leaderscampfire.com
"An Hour A Week?" www.cubmasterchris.com
"Cubcast" www.scouting.org/cubscouts/podcast/index.html
"Small pack Leader" www.smallpackleader.com
"BSA Podcast" wgrasse.libsyn.com/
"The Adventures of a Cub Scout Parent and Cubmaster" odeo.com/channel/487/view/

Discussion Groups

I highly recommend that you join a Yahoo Group. It's free to join and you'll meet some of the nicest people around! People share helpful ideas and tips in a real-time setting. You can receive the emails individually or as a daily digest. Some groups are more active than others, so the quantity of e-mails will vary.

Appendix 1

Yahoo Groups:

Ldsactivitydays	PriPres
StakePrimary	LDSsharing
PrimaryPage	CluelessLDSPrimaryPresidents
PrimaryST	ldsprimarykids
Lds_CSL	Cub-Scout-Talk
craftingLDS	ldvprimary at http://latter-dayvillage.com

Clip Art

I'm thankful for talented artists who share their wonderful creations with me, since I have trouble even drawing stick people! Here are some of those generous artists who share their talents. Many of the websites mentioned above include great artwork too.

http://www.lds.org/gospellibrary/pdfmagazine/0,7779,594-7-1-2001,00.html# The *Friend* magazines from January 2001 with all photos and illustrations

http://lds.mycityport.com/

www.christysclipart.com

http://www.graphicgarden.com/

www.debanae.net

http://designca.com/lds/

www.coloringbookfun.com

www.stums.org/closet/html/index.html

http://www.oneil.com.au/lds/pictures.html

http://lds.about.com/library/gallery/clipart/blclipart_gallery_subindex.htm

www.free-clip-art.net

www.ldsfiles.com/clipart

www.kidsdomain.com/clip/

Appendix 2:

Primary's Faith in God and Cub Scout Equivalents

Primary's Faith in God program requirements:	Cub Scout equivalents:

Learning and Living the Gospel
Complete at least two of the following activities each year:

1. Explain how taking the sacrament helps you renew your baptismal covenant. In a family home evening, teach others about things we can do to remain faithful.	Wolf Achievement #11 Bear Achievement #1 Part of Webelo's Family Member #5 Webelo's Badge requirement #8
2. Give a family home evening lesson on Joseph's Smith First Vision (see Joseph Smith- History 1:1-20). Discuss how Heavenly Father answers our sincere prayers. * **Cub Scout Religious Patch requirement**	Wolf-Achievement 11 (page 94) Wolf Elective 22c Bear-Achievement 1a (page 27) Webelo's "Family Member" 5 (page 227) Communicating belt loop requirement #1

Appendix 2

3. Mark these verses about the Holy Ghost in your scriptures: John 14:16–17, 2 Nephi 32:5, and Moroni 10:5. Discuss ways the Holy Ghost helps you.	Wolf Achievement #11 Webelos badge requirement 8e (3rd one)
4. Read a recent conference address given by the prophet. Decide what you can do to follow the prophet, and do it.	Wolf Achievement #11 Bear achievements 1b, 18a Webelos badge requirement 8e (3rd one)
5. Give an opening and a closing prayer in family home evening or at Primary. Share your feelings about how prayer protects us and helps us to stay close to Heavenly Father and the Savior. * **Cub Scout Religious Patch requirement**	Wolf Achievement 11 (page 94) Part of Bear Achievement 1 (page 26) Webelo's "Family Member" #5 (page 227)
6. Tell a story from the Book of Mormon that teaches about faith in Jesus Christ. Share your testimony of the Savior. * **Cub Scout Religious Patch requirement**	Wolf Achievement 11a Wolf-Arrow point 22c (page 220) Bear Achievement 1a Webelos badge requirement #8a Communicating belt loop requirement #1
7. Read D&C 89. Discuss how Heavenly Father blesses us when we faithfully live the Word of Wisdom. Help plan and conduct an activity to teach the Word of Wisdom to others.	Wolf achievement 3a, 12b Bear Achievement 9d Webelo's Communicator #2 Webelo's Fitness 4, 5, 6, 7 and 8 Physical Fitness belt loop requirement #1

Appendix 2

8. Prepare a pedigree chart with your name and your parents' and grandparents' names. Prepare a family group record for your family and share a family story. Discuss how performing temple work blesses families. * **Cub Scout Religious Patch requirement**	Wolf-Achievement 11 (page 94) Bear Achievement 8d, 18f Webelo's Family Member #12 Heritages belt loop and pin
9. Learn to sing "Choose the Right" (Hymns, no. 239). Explain what agency is and what it means to be responsible for your choices. Discuss how making good choices has helped you develop greater faith.	Wolf achievements 9a and 12 Wolf Elective #11d and e Bear achievements 1b and 24e Webelo's Handyman requirement #1 Music Belt loop #2 Citizen pin requirement #7
10. Plan and complete your own activity that will help you learn and live the gospel	Use any of the fun ideas in Chapter 5!

Serving Others

Complete at least two of the following activities each year:

1. Read and discuss the parable of the good Samaritan (see Luke 10:30–37). Plan and complete a service project that helps a family member or neighbor. After completing the project, discuss how it helped your faith grow stronger.	Wolf Achievement 7d Bear Achievement 6g Part of Webelo's Family member #5 Webelo's Scholar 3 and 13 Webelo's badge requirements 8e (5th one) Citizen belt loop requirement #3

Appendix 2

2. Write a letter to a teacher, your parents, or your grandparents telling them what you appreciate and respect about them. * **Cub Scout Religious Patch requirement**	If you use a computer—Wolf elective #21b Bear Achievement 18b,e and 24d Webelo's "Communicator" 11 (page 165) Communicating belt loop requirement 2
3. Make a list of the qualities you like in a person. Choose one quality to develop in yourself. Discuss how showing respect and kindness strengthens you, your family, and others.	Wolf Achievement 6a,7a,e,9a,10a Bear Achievements 8g and 24f Webelos Naturalist #1 Webelos Scholar #1
4. Plan, prepare, and serve a nutritious meal.	Wolf Achievement #8 Bear Achievement 9c,g Part of Webelo's Family Member #11 Webelos Fitness #3 Heritages pin requirement #9
5. Entertain young children with songs or games you have learned or made yourself. Show that you know how to care for and protect a young child.	Wolf Achievement 10b Wolf elective 4 Bear Achievement 10b Webelos Family Member 8 Communicating pin requirement 10
6. Learn about and practice good manners and courtesy.	Wolf Achievement 4c,10a Bear achievement 24d

APPENDIX 2

7. Plan and hold a parent-child activity, such as a dinner, picnic, hike, day trip, or service project.	Wolf Achievements 4f, 8c,e and 10 Wolf electives 18 a,b,c,d,e and 19c Bear Achievements 10 ; 12; 14g; 15a Bear Elective 16d Webelos Family Member #8 Webelos Outdoorsman #2 Citizen pin requirement #10 Heritages Pin requirement #2 Wildlife Conservation pin requirement #8
8. Read the twelfth article of faith. Discuss what it means to be a good citizen and how your actions can affect others.	Wolf Achievement 2 Wolf Electives 11a,b Bear Achievement 3j Webelos Citizen 1,4,7,8,9,12,13,14,15 Citizenship belt loop and pin
9. Help your Primary leaders plan and carry out an upcoming quarterly activity. * Cub Scout Religious Patch requirement	Wolf Achievement 11d Wolf Elective 9a (page 152) Bear Achievement 24c (page 176) If the Primary activity is a service project, this can also be part of the Citizenship beltoop requirement #3
10. Plan and complete your own activity to serve others.	Use any of the ideas in Chapter 6!

Developing Talents

Complete at least two of the following activities each year:

1. Learn how to budget and save money. Discuss why it is important to faithfully pay our tithing and how Heavenly Father blesses us when we do (see 3 Nephi 24:10–11).	Bear Achievement 13c,g Bear Elective 21 Webelos Family Member 3, 4, 7, 8

APPENDIX 2

2. Pay your tithing and begin saving for a mission.	Bear Achievement 13b
3. Learn to sing, play, or lead a song from the Children's Songbook. Teach or share the song in a family home evening or at Primary. Discuss how developing talents helps prepare us for service to Heavenly Father and others.	Wolf Electives 11 d,e and f Part of Bear Achievement 1b Bear Electives 8b and d Webelos Showman 8,9,14 Music belt loop #2 Music pin #2 and #7
4. Write a poem, story, or short play that teaches a principle of the gospel or is about Heavenly Father's creations. * **Cub Scout Religious Patch requirement**	Wolf-Achievement 11 (page 94) Wolf Electives 2 and 21b Bear Achievement 18f (page 144) Could be Webelo's Showman 2 or 19 Communicating pin requirement #1,6
5. Make an item from wood, metal, fabric, or other material, or draw, paint, or sculpt a piece of art. Display your finished work for others to see.	Wolf Achievement 5e; Wolf Electives 3a; 5b,c,d,e,f,g,h,i; 7b,c; 8d; 9b,c; 10b,c,d,e; 12a,b,d,e,f; Bear Achievements 5b, 19c, 20b, 21a,b,d,f; Bear Electives 1b,d, 2b,c; 6d,g; 8a, 9a,c; 10,12,18b; Webelo's Artist 3, 5,6,7,8,9,10,11; Webelos Craftman; Webelos Engineer 7,8,9; Art belt loop and pin; Communicating belt loop requirements #3; Citizen belt loop req #2; Citizen pin req #3; Heritages belt loop req #2; Heritages pin req #8; Wildlife Conservation pin req #5; Pinewood Derby; Raingutter Regatta

147

Appendix 2

6. Visit an art museum or attend a concert, play, or other cultural event. Share your experience with your family or activity day group.	Wolf Achievement 10f Bear Achievement 10a Bear Elective 9b Webelos Showman 17 Webelos Traveler 4 Music pin requirement #6 Art pin requirement #1
7. Read D&C 88:118. Discuss what it means to "seek learning, even by study and also by faith." Improve your personal study habits by doing such things as learning how to choose and read good books or being prepared for school each day.	Wolf Elective 6b Webelos Scholar 2,4,5
8. List five things you can do to help around your home. Discuss the importance of obeying and honoring your parents and learning how to work	Wolf Achievements 4a,d,e; 7f; 9b,c; Wolf Electives 14a; 15a,b,c,d; 16; Bear Achievements 7e, 11, 13a, 16a, 18a; Bear Electives 17 and 21b Webelos Family Member 2,9,10,11,13; Webelos Handyman; Webelos Readyman Citizen belt loop req #1; Citizen pin req #4

APPENDIX 2

9. Plan a physical fitness program for yourself that may include learning to play a sport or game. Participate in the program for one month.	Wolf achievement 1a, h, j; Wolf elective 20; Bear Achievements 14b,f; 15a, 16, 18c, 23a,b,c; Bear Elective 20 Webelos Athlete; Webelos Sportsman 2,3,4; Physical Fitness belt loop and pin; Other Sport belt loops and pins
10. Learn about and practice good nutrition, good health, and good grooming, including modest dress.	Wolf achievement 3a Bear Achievement 9d Webelos Athlete 2,3 Webelos Fitness 1,3,4 Physical Fitness pin req. #1
11. Plan and complete your own activity that will help you develop your talents	Use any of the ideas in Chapter 7!

Preparing for the Priesthood

Complete the following activities while you are 11 years old. They will help you prepare to receive the Aaronic Priesthood and become a righteous young man.

1. Learn about the restoration of the Aaronic Priesthood (see D&C 13, D&C 107:20, and Joseph Smith—History 1:68–73).	The Religious Knot Award needs to be earned before a boy turns 11 years old, so these priesthood-related requirements do not have Cub Scout equivalents. In the Church, the boys advance to the "11 Year Old Scout" program while still in Primary.

Appendix 2

2. Read D&C 20:57–60 and Aaronic Priesthood: Fulfilling Our Duty to God [Deacon], page 7. Discuss with a parent or leader the purposes of the Aaronic Priesthood and what it means to do your duty to God.	
3. Talk with the deacons quorum presidency about the role of the deacons quorum. Write in your journal how you can serve the Lord as a member of a deacons quorum.	
4. Read D&C 88:77–80, D&C 88:118 and D&C 130:19. Discuss with a parent or Primary leader how important a good education is and how it can help strengthen you as a priesthood holder in your home and family and in the Church.	
5. Read "The Family: A Proclamation to the World." Make a list of things you can do to help strengthen your family and make a happy home. Share the list with your parents or Primary leader.	

APPENDIX 2

To earn the Primary's Faith in God Award, you also need to complete the following:

Basic Requirements for the Primary's Faith in God Award for Boys	
1. Pray daily to Heavenly Father. 2. Read the scriptures regularly. 3. Keep the commandments and live "My Gospel Standards" 4. Honor your parents and be kind to your family. 5. Pay your tithing and attend tithing settlement. 6. Attend sacrament meetings and Primary regularly.	Wolf Achievement 11 Bear Achievement 1 Webelo's Badge requirement 8
Other Requirements 1. Write your testimony. 2. Memorize the Articles of Faith and explain what they mean. 3. Have an interview with a member of your bishopric or branch presidency	

Appendix 3:
Passing Off Requirements

Most requirements in Cub Scouts can be passed off at home by a parent, called "Akela." Many parents believe that it's the responsibility of the Cub Scout leader to pass everything off and help their son advance. In reality, it's the other way around—Cub Scout leaders are there to support the parents' guidance in helping their son advance! You will see by the list below that there are very few requirements that cannot be done at home with a parent.

Requirements that have to be passed off with the Den or Pack

Wolf Achievement 2b, e
Wolf Elective 3f
Wolf Elective 11f
Wolf Elective 12f
Wolf Elective 14c,
Wolf Elective 18f
Wolf Elective 20c, n, o
Wolf Elective 23a, g, e, f

Bear Achievement 3f, h, i
Bear Achievement 4c
Bear Achievement 6g
Bear Achievement 15b, c
Bear Achievement 24a, b, c
Bear Elective 8c
Bear Elective 9a
Bear Elective 13b

Webelos Badge #6
Webelos Badge—Troop meeting
Webelos Badge—Scoutmaster Conference
Webelos Badge—Conservation or service project
Webelos Aquanaut 7
Webelos Citizenship 3
Webelos Communicator 2, 4, 5, 9, 10

Appendix 3

Webelos Outdoorsman 4, 6, 9, 12
Webelos Showman 1, 5, 6

Wolf activities that can be done and passed off at home

Achievements:
 1a, b, c, d, e, f, g, h, i, j, k, l
 2a, c, d, g
 3a, b, c
 4a, b, c, d, e, f
 5a, b, c, d, e
 6a, b, c
 7a, b, c, d, e, f
 8a, b, c, d, e
 9a, b, c, d, e
 10a, b, c, d, e, f, g
 11a, b, c, d
 12a, b, c, d, e, f, g, h, i, j, k

Electives:
 1a, b, c, d
 2a, b, c, d, e
 3a, b, c, d, e
 4a, b, c, d, e
 5a, b, c, d, e, f, g, h, i
 6a, b, c
 7a, b, c
 8a, b, c, d
 9a, b, c
 10a, b, c, d, e, f
 11a, b, c, d, e
 12a, b, d, e
 13a, b, c, d, e, f
 14a, b, d
 15a, b, c, d, e
 16a, b, c
 17a, b, c, d, e, f, g
 18a, b, c, d, e, g
 19a, b, c, d, e, f
 20a, b, d, e, f, g, h, I, j, k, l, m
 21a, b, c
 22a, b, c, d, e

Bear activities that can be done and passed off at home

Achievements:
 1a, b
 2
 3a, b, c, d
 4a, b, c
 5a, b, c, d, e
 6a, b, c, d, e, f
 7a, c, d, e, f
 8a, b, c, d, e, f, g
 9a, b, c, d, e, f, g
 10a, b
 11a, b, c, d, e, f, g
 12a, b, c, d, e
 13a, b, c, d, e, f, g
 14a, b, c, d, e, f, g
 15a

Appendix 3

16a, b
17a, b, c, d, e, f, g, h
18a, b, c, d, e, f, g, h
19a, b, c, d
20a, b, c
21a, b, c, d, e, f, g
22a, b, c, d, e, f
23a, b, c, d, e
24a, d, e, f

Electives:
1a, b, c, d, e, f
2a, b, c, d, e, f
3a, b
4a, b, c, d, e
5a, b, c, d, e
6a, b, c, d, e, f, g
7a, b, c, d
8a, b, d
9b, c
10a, b, c
11a, b, c, d
12a, b, c, d, e, f, g, h
13a, c, d

Webelos requirements that can be passed off at home

Webelos Badge 1, 2, 3, 4, 5, 7, 7, 8
Aquanaut 1, 2, 3, 4, 5, 6, 8
Artist 1, 2, 3, 4, 5, 6, 7, 8, 9, 10, 11
Athlete 1, 2, 3, 4, 5, 6, 7, 8, 9
Citizen 1, 2, 3, 4, 5, 6, 7, 9, 10, 12, 13, 14, 15, 16, 17
Communicator 1, 3, 6, 7, 8, 11, 12, 13, 14, 15, 16
Craftsman 1, 2, 3, 4
Engineer 1, 2, 3, 4, 5, 6, 7, 8, 9, 10
Family Member 1, 2, 3, 4, 5, 6, 7, 8, 9, 10, 11, 12, 13 (Most of these *have* to be done at home!)
Fitness 1, 2, 5, 6, 7, 8
Forester 1, 2, 3, 4, 5, 6, 7, 8, 9, 10
Geologist 1, 2, 3, 4, 5, 6, 7, 9
Handyman 1, 2, 3, 4, 5, 6, 7, 8, 9, 10, 11, 12, 13, 14, 15, 16, 17
Naturalist 1, 2, 3, 5, 6, 7, 8, 9, 10, 12
Outdoorsman 1, 2, 7, 8, 10, 11
Readyman 1, 2, 3, 4, 5, 6, 7, 8, 9, 10, 11, 12, 13, 14
Scholar 1, 2, 3, 4, 5, 6, 7, 8, 9, 10, 11, 12, 13
Scientist 1, 2, 3, 4, 5, 6, 7, 8, 9, 10, 11, 12, 13, 14
Showman 1, 2, 3, 4, 7, 8, 9, 10, 11, 12, 13, 14, 15, 18, 19, 20, 21, 22, 23
Sportsman 1, 2, 3, 4
Traveler 1, 2, 3, 5, 6, 8, 9, 10, 11, 12, 13

Index

Activities

A
animal shelter 63
Articles of Faith 46–49, 52, 53
Ask the Scriptures 53

B
bake bread 20, 28, 80
bike safety 39, 73
birds 45, 79
board game 44, 55
book club 72
Book of Mormon 43, 45, 57, 108, 133
Book of Mormon, map of 27
building blocks 44

C
calendar 36, 50, 58, 97, 99, 100
calligraphy 22, 38, 43
campout 37, 45, 78, 91
candle 11
candles 55
carnival 48
Character Connections 53, 55
chimes 54
city hall 77, 82
collage 16
Concentration 15
Congressman 64
Cranium 55
cross-stitch 11, 30
crossword puzzle 48, 117

D
dance 66, 83
divine nature 10
door hangers 19, 30
Dutch oven 78

INDEX

E
emergency preparedness 56

F
Family History Center 35
family traditions 34, 103
fashion show 30
fishing 26, 75
flags 60, 71, 104, 121
flannel board stories 55
font, cleaning of 19, 20
food storage 54, 63

G
game show 55
garden 79, 113
gospel craft 52
greeting cards 36

H
handiwork 11
hangman 27
healthy habits 9, 10, 84
House Olympics 71

I
illustrations 28, 141

J
Jeopardy 49, 55
journal 24, 39, 44, 45, 91, 140, 150
Jungle Book 33

K
karaoke 54
Kindness Cans 33
knots 24, 26, 79

L
lanyard 48
letter writing 14, 22, 37, 39, 46, 69, 75, 88, 90, 101, 102, 134, 145
library 28, 72
literacy 66
Lorenzo Snow 41
luncheon 66

M
magazines 9, 11, 141
magic tricks 73
masks 15, 25
melodrama 71
mirror 12
missionaries 17, 26, 27, 31, 43, 45, 62, 67, 81, 108, 115, 131

mobiles 31
musical instruments 22
music video 83

N

nature hike 9, 74
necktie 42, 89
nursery 53, 68

O

obstacle course 26, 27

P

pen pals 30, 109
photo album 11, 91
physical fitness 86, 149
piggy bank 40
pillow cases 30
place mats 37, 118
planetarium 11
podcast 52, 140
police station 79
pool 84
poster 12, 13, 31, 36, 47, 73, 82
Prayer Rocks 21
pretzel 21
Priesthood Preview 88
progressive dinner 10
puppets 18, 24, 25, 30, 40

Q

quilt 65, 97

R

rag rugs 22
raisins 29
recipes 16, 25, 54, 55, 103
recycling center 80
Red Cross 58, 65, 114
retirement home 67

S

sacrament 15, 42, 80, 92, 105, 132
Sacred Grove experience 45
sand art 45
Scout Spirit 68
scrapbook 18, 38, 44, 102, 105
scripture stories 25, 28, 47
sculpture 23, 27, 78
seat covers 81
secret language 23
service coupon 67
service project 58, 60, 61, 69, 104, 107, 127, 144, 146, 152
Sharing Time 10, 13, 15, 19, 22, 24, 31, 76, 116, 132
shrink art 26, 31
sign language 64
skits 123, 128, 136

Index

slide show 18
soap 17
stilts 78
Stump the Bishop 53
Sunday Bag 42

T

tacky night 11
tithing settlement 40, 51, 151
travel box 81
trivia 54

U

unusual sports 84

V

Velveteen Rabbit 13

Y

yard work 62, 65, 68, 102

Z

zoo 78, 84

* **To see more Cub Scout ideas and helpful index resources that didn't fit into this book, go to Trina's website at www.boicebox.com**

About the Author

Trina Boice is a native Californian who currently lives in Las Vegas. In 2004 she was honored as the California Young Mother of the Year, an award which completely amuses her four sons. She earned two Bachelor's degrees from BYU, where she competed on the Speech and Debate team and the Ballroom Dance Team, winning national titles for both teams.

She has a real estate license, travel agent license, two master's degrees, and a black belt in Tae Kwon Do, although she's the first one to admit she'd pass out from fright if she were ever really attacked by a bad guy.

Trina currently writes for Roots Television and Go2.com and is the executive marketing director for Multi-Pure International. Trina was selected by KPBS in San Diego to be a political correspondent during the last election year. If she told you what she really did, she'd have to kill you.

A popular and entertaining speaker, Trina is the author of seven books and can't wait to write her next one! You can read more about her other books at www.boicebox.com.

Trina is currently serving as Cubmaster for her youngest son's pack in Las Vegas!

12-20

0 26575 53528 0

JEFFERSON COUNTY PUBLIC LIBRARY